# Robots

GREAT INVENTIONS

# Robots

R E B E C C A   S T E F O F F

 **Marshall Cavendish**
Benchmark

New York

*This book is for Stephen Kechley, friend and fellow science-fiction fan.*

Marshall Cavendish Benchmark
99 White Plains Road
Tarrytown, NY 10591-9001
www.marshallcavendish.us

Stefoff, Rebecca, [date]
Robots / by Rebecca Stefoff.
p. cm. — (Great inventions)
Includes bibliographical references and index.
ISBN 978-0-7614-2601-1
1. Robots.  I. Title.
TJ211.15.S74 2007
629.8'92—dc22
2007011388

Publisher: Michelle Bisson
Art Director: Anahid Hamparian
Series design by Sonia Chaghatzbanian

Photo research by Candlepants Incorporated

Cover Photo: Malte Christians / Getty Images
Title page: Actress Brigitte Helm portrayed the first robot ever seen on film in
Fritz Lang's 1926 movie *Metropolis*.

The photographs in this book are used by permission and through the courtesy of:
*Corbis*: Bettmann, 2, 44, 93; Digital Art, 8, 70, back cover; Forrest J. Ackerman Collection, 11; Ralph White,
84; Gabe Palmer, 116. *Kobal*: C-2 Pictures/Warner Bros./The Kobal Collection/Robert Zuckerman, 13. *The Image
Works*: Albert Harlingue/Roger-Viollet, 16; Mary Evans Picture Library, 24, 27, 49; sspl, 53; Twentieth Century
Fox/Topham, 58; Norbert von der Groeben, 112; Fujifotos, 98-99, 119; Ann Ronan Picture Library, 121;
Jim Sulley/Newscast, 124. *The Bridgeman Art Library*: ©Galleria Spada, Rome, Italy/ Alinari, 20. *Art Resource,
NY*: Werner Forman, 22. *Getty Images*: John Kobal Foundation, 29; Edward G Malindine, 32; Boyer/Roger
Viollet, 36; Steve Dunwell, 38; Hulton Archive, 41; Seth Resnick, 46; Frank Capri, 51; Ralph S. Mosher Yale
Joel/Time & Life Pictures, 56; David Paul Morris, 63; Greg Wood, 65; Doug McFadd, 67; AFP, 79; Chip
Somodevilla, 81; Bill Ingalls, 86; Garry Gay, 90; Malte Christians, 97; Louie Psihoyos, 102. *Photo Researchers
Inc.*: Sam Ogden, 60; Pascal Goetgheluck, 76-77. Super Stock: age fotostock, 73; Stockdisc, 95; Roger Harris,
108-109. *AP Images*: NASA, 88.

Printed in Malaysia

1 3 5 6 4 2

# Contents

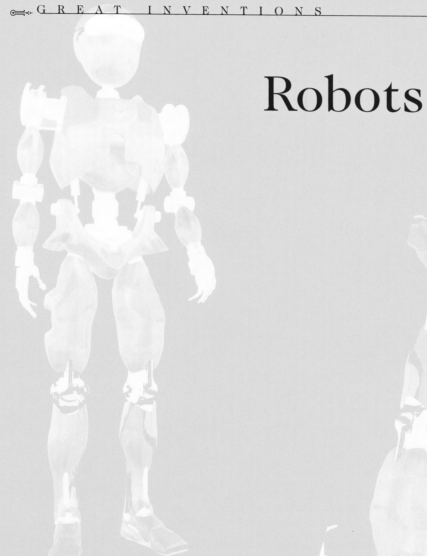

# Robots

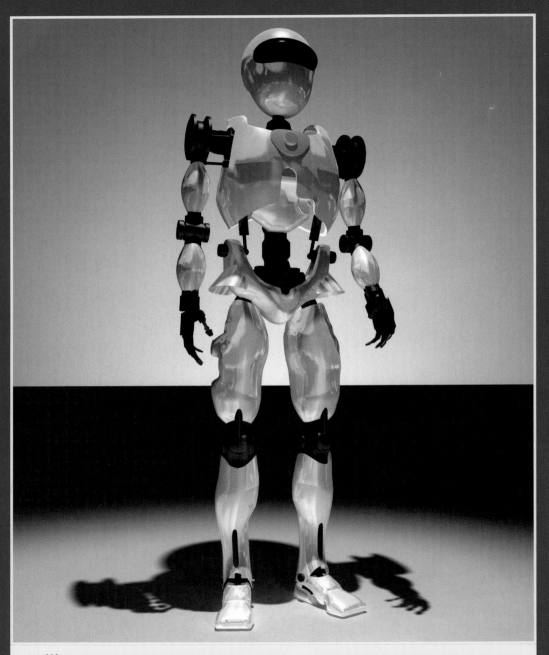

When you imagine a robot, you may picture a machine shaped something like a person. The great majority of robots in the world today, though, look much less human than this vision of a humanoid robot.

# Robot Dreams, Robot Nightmares

Flying cars cruise among the tops of the city's towers, flashing in the sunlight. The cars have passengers, but no drivers—each car drives itself. Inside the towers, robot attendants give care and companionship to the elderly, help children with their homework, serve perfectly cooked dinners, and don't complain afterward about doing the dishes. Beneath the streets, a sewer line has ruptured, but the dirty, dangerous work of repairing it is in the capable hands of mechanical laborers who are immune to germs and fatigue. Freed from worry and work by their mechanical servants, the people of the city can devote themselves to learning, art, and enjoyment.

That's one vision of the future. In another, choking clouds of dust and ash swirl above a scorched, war-torn landscape. Heavy footsteps shake the ground, and the drone of machinery fills the air. The last humans scurry like desperate rats, diving into tunnels to hide from the all-knowing, all-powerful mechanical monsters that stalk the land and patrol the skies, seeking to wipe out the remnants of their flesh-and-blood creators. The robots have turned against us, and they're winning the war.

These visions are just science fiction. At the beginning of the twenty-first century, robots are a long way from taking over the world. But they *are* vacuuming our floors, exploring our neighboring planets, battling each other in arenas, and even helping surgeons perform delicate operations on us. At this moment, engineers in robotics labs and tinkerers in garages are building new robots with advanced capabilities. Robots are becoming more useful, and more powerful, all the time.

Our images of robots come largely from science fiction. They span a vast variety of forms and behaviors, including the lumbering, droning mechanical man known as Robby the Robot in the 1956 movie *Forbidden Planet*; the chirping, beeping R2D2 and the timid, worry-prone C3PO of *Star Wars*; Data, the artificial man who yearns to experience human emotions on the television series *Star Trek: The Next Generation;* and the deadly, time-traveling killer robots of the *Terminator* films. These and other entertainments have introduced the public to some of the many forms robots may take.

Robby and C3PO, for example, are what robotics experts call humanoid robots, built in the shape of human beings. Robby's resemblance is pretty basic—just two legs, two arms, and a "head" that is a glass dome through which moving parts can be seen. C3PO is more human in shape and motion, with a head on which twin cameras and a speaker grid are arranged like eyes and a mouth.

The Terminator is different. Covered with flesh, it looks completely human (although eerily expressionless), until the flesh burns away, revealing the metallic skeleton within. Some robot scientists would classify the Terminator as a cyborg, or cybernetic organism—an entity in which flesh-and-blood organic parts are combined with mechanical parts. The central character of the *Robocop* films is also a cyborg. He is a human police officer who, after being fatally wounded, is rebuilt with robotic parts but retains his human face and his memories. Another well-known cyborg is the Tin Man in L. Frank Baum's 1900 novel *The Wonderful Wizard of Oz.* The Tin Man was a human woodcutter who replaced various body parts with tin replicas after a series of mishaps with an enchanted ax. Seven years later, in *Ozma of Oz,* Baum wrote about a true robot, an emotionless copper servant called Tiktok that runs by clockwork.

*Star Trek*'s Data, in contrast, is an android, a robot that is completely

An old magazine cover illustrates a long-lasting theme in fiction about robots—the fear that intelligent, powerful machines may one day destroy the human race.

artificial but is made to look and act as human as possible. The term *android* has been used with a wide degree of variation, however. Sometimes, as in the *Star Wars* movies (where the term is shortened to "droid"), it applies to any kind of robot.

Unlike the Terminator or Data, none of today's real-life robots can pass for human, although some of them have body structures and basic facial expressions that resemble ours. The majority of robots, however, are not shaped anything like a human being. These robots are designed not to imitate a person but to perform certain tasks. Depending upon their purposes, they can look like spiders, snakes, disembodied arms, toy tanks, dogs, featureless disks, or—in the no-holds-barred world of robot arena sports—mobile, aggressive buzz saws.

So what is a robot? There are almost as many definitions as there are designs. Many roboticists—the scientists and engineers who design and work with robots—say that any definition of a robot starts with three basic elements: a moving, motor-driven body; some form of sensing capability that lets the robot perceive the world around it; and a "brain" that directs its actions, usually in the form of a computer program. An ordinary car moves, but it is not a robot, even if it is equipped with a computer that provides directions and controls the interior environment, because it must be operated by a driver inside the car.

Under certain circumstances, though, a car can become a kind of robot. For movie stunts and safety tests, automobiles can be fitted with remote-control devices so that they can be driven from a distance. A car being manipulated in this way may appear to be driving itself, but in reality it is being teleoperated. A teleoperated device is controlled by a human operator who directs the device's actions by using a video game–style joystick, a keyboard, voice commands, or some other kind of control system. The operator's instructions are communicated to the device by a cable or as broadcast signals. Teleoperated devices are sometimes called telerobots. Many of the robots now used in industry, medicine, engineering, and scientific exploration fall into this category. Autonomous or self-directed robots, unlike telerobots, are capable of

As a cybernetic creation from the future, Arnold Schwarzenegger was part flesh and part metal in the *Terminator* movie trilogy.

fully independent action, although that action may be as simple as rolling around on the floor sucking up cat hair.

A computer by itself is not a robot because it does not move and act. In 1997, for example, a computer program called Deep Blue defeated world chess champion Gary Kasparov, but Deep Blue was not a robot. It calculated the moves of the game, but someone had to move the chess pieces for it. Since that time, however, many people have created autonomous robots that play chess against human opponents. These robots move their own pawns, bishops, and other pieces on the chessboard. Most of them take the form of mechanical arms driven by computers.

A simple chess-playing robot shows how complicated it can be to create a robot to do just one thing. First, the robot must know how to play chess. Many computer programs for chess are available commercially, so the robot's creator does not have to write a chess-playing program from scratch—but he or she does have to write the program that connects the chess program to the programs that govern the robot's physical operations. Second, the robot must be able to perceive the board and the moves of the pieces. To do so, it needs a sensor, such as a camera, that is coupled with a recognition program. This program must identify each square on the board as dark or light; it must also identify the shape of each piece and its position. Third, the robot has to be able to move its chess pieces. This calls for some kind of "hand," perhaps a pincer on an extendable, rotating arm. The hand must be equipped with force sensors so that the robot knows when it has grasped a chess piece—and knows when to stop tightening its grip, so that it doesn't crush the piece. The hand must be able to lower itself, close its grip, move the piece to a new location, release its grip, and move up and out of the way without knocking over the other pieces. Making a robot that can play chess is no easy task. We probably do not have to worry for some time yet about a robot that can take over the world.

Dictionary definitions of robots over the years have focused on two points. One point is that a robot is a machine designed to function in place of a human being, or to perform actions that are normally done by humans. The second point is that a robot operates with little outside control and, because of its design and programming, gives the appearance of having at least some independence and intelligence. These twin concepts—that a robot is a substitute for a person, and that a robot can act independently and with purpose—form the basis of *R.U.R.*, a play written in 1920 by a Czech writer named Karel Capek. The play was staged in Prague, Czechoslovakia, in 1921. The following year, translated into English, it appeared in New York City. Throughout the 1920s, *R.U.R.* played in many countries, introducing audiences to a new word: *robot*.

*R.U.R.* stands for "Rossum's Universal Robots." The play marked the first use of the word *robot*. The word was not Capek's creation; his brother Josef had suggested it to him. In Czech and some other Slavic languages, *robota* means "servitude" or "forced labor." The term *robotnik* had come into use to describe peasants, factory workers, or others who performed mindless drudgery. Capek shortened this term to *robot* and gave it a new twist, applying it to beings that had been created to serve humans as laborers.

Capek's robots were not mechanical constructs, even though the actors who played them on stage were generally outfitted with metallic, machinelike costumes. According to references in the play, the robots are made out of an artificial form of flesh that is manufactured in vats and then stamped or pressed into a humanlike form. Capek does not explain how these creations were endowed with motion, speech, and the ability to work, but giving a plausible scientific basis for robotics is not the point. Capek's purpose is to examine the question of what it means to be human. As an author, Capek once said, he was more interested in people than in robots.

In *R.U.R.*, the Rossum's Universal Robots company is selling its products to factory owners and employers who are replacing human workers with these efficient new creations. One character explains that the best kind of worker is the cheapest one, the one with the fewest

MARIA THE *METROPOLIS* ROBOT WAS BUILT BY A SCIENTIST (CENTER) WHO PLANNED TO GIVE IT THE APPEARANCE OF A WOMAN HE HAD LOVED. A RUTHLESS POLITICAL LEADER (LEFT) INSTEAD USES THE ROBOT AS A PAWN IN THE CONFLICT BETWEEN THE TWO FACTIONS OF FUTURE SOCIETY—THE THINKERS AND THE WORKERS.

needs. The Rossum father-and-son team of robot makers produces highly efficient workers by eliminating from their makeup everything that is not related to work. As the play opens, a young woman named Helena Glory travels to the Rossum factory. She believes that the robots should not be enslaved; her goal is to free them. At her request, one of the scientists at the factory alters some of the robots. Helena thinks that the changes will let the robots develop into true people, with feelings and souls. Her plan works, but—as so often happens in tales about secret laboratories where scientists tamper with the very fabric of life itself—it produces unexpected consequences.

One of the altered robots acquires the human feelings of rage, rebelliousness, and ambition. He issues a command: "Robots of the world, you are ordered to exterminate the human race." Robots take over the factory and kill all but one of the humans. Before her death, Helena destroys the secret formula for robot manufacture. Without it, the newly dominant robots cannot make more of their own kind; to their dismay, the factory now turns out "nothing but bloody chunks of meat." In the end, Helena's humanizing modifications produce another unexpected result: Two of the robots fall in love. The sole surviving human gives these two robots the names Adam and Eve and sends them out into the world to make a fresh start.

Capek, who died in 1939, considered *R.U.R.* one of his least interesting pieces of writing, but it became his most famous work. Some people interpreted *R.U.R.* as a political or economic allegory, a story that shows how the humanity of workers is stripped away by a system that treats them as pieces of machinery, valued only for their efficiency. Others saw it as a warning of the terrible power that may be unleashed when the oppressed masses rise up against those who control them. On a philosophical level, *R.U.R.* suggests that perhaps the indefinable spark of humanity dwells in how beings feel and act, not in how they are created, and that human nature is composed of violence and hatred as well as tenderness and love.

The themes that Capek wove into *R.U.R.* have been explored in many later works of robot-related fiction. These themes include the ethics of creating artificial life, possible uses (and misuses) of robots, the differences and similarities between humans and robots, robots becoming human, and robots destroying their creators. In 1926, for example, German filmmaker Fritz Lang released *Metropolis*, a silent film that is both a political fable and an early science-fiction tale. Set in the year 2026, *Metropolis* is the story of an idealistic woman named Maria, who, like Capek's Helena, dedicates herself to helping the oppressed working class. The evil oppressors, however, create a robot—the first to appear on film. They give the robot Maria's appearance and use it to create discord and confusion among the workers, who eventually burn it at the stake. The movie's plot was based on the idea that advanced science could create a robot that would successfully impersonate a human being.

Although the word *robot* originated in the early twentieth century, the vision of an artificial human is very ancient. Myths and legends from many times and places capture the uneasy tension between the human urge to create tools and servants in our own image, and the fear that if these servants are too much like us, with minds and wills of their own, we will be unable to control them.

# Myths and Mechanical Marvels

The god Hephaestos, said the ancient Greeks, was a metal-smith of divine skill. Working in his fiery forge beneath a volcano, Hephaestos built companions and servants for himself. The Greek epic poem *The Iliad* describes them: maidens made of gold, who were not merely beautiful but also wise, and tables and stools with wheeled feet that moved around on their own. Hephaestos's mythic creations certainly sound like robots.

The ingenious inventor Daedalus, another figure from Greek legend, is said to have constructed statues so real that they tried to run away. Similar lifelike statues populate the legends of many countries; sometimes they are described as clever mechanical devices, while at other times they are ordinary statues that come to life through the action of magic or the gods. Legends tell of sages in ancient India who made walking mechanical men and elephants out of wood. An old Chinese story recounts the adventures of a prince who made a moving wooden man so lifelike that a queen started to fall in love with it until the prince pulled a bolt out of the mechanism and the whole thing collapsed into a pile of sticks. Early Jewish folklore featured the *golem*, a manlike creature made of mud or earth that could be brought to life by a holy mystic.

Some of the Greeks and Romans who traveled in ancient Egypt reported that temples there contained statues of the gods that answered

DAEDALUS, A MASTER INVENTOR IN ANCIENT GREEK AND ROMAN MYTHOLOGY, FABRICATES A MECHANICAL COW IN AN ANCIENT ROMAN SCULPTURE. THE IDEA OF ARTIFICIAL CREATIONS THAT IMITATE LIVING BEINGS APPEARS IN THE MYTHS AND OLD TALES OF MANY CULTURES.

questions from worshippers by speaking or moving their heads or hands. Even in ancient times, people speculated on the mechanisms by which the priests could have manipulated these "living statues." Hidden speaking tubes might have carried someone's voice from another room into the mouth of a statue; such a tube could have the added benefit of making the voice sound deep, hollow, and eerie. If statues had been crafted with the proper joints, concealed operators could have caused the statues' heads or arms to move by means of levers.

Archaeologists have found old masks and puppets with movable jaws and built-in speaking tubes in Egypt, India, and southeastern Asia. These objects were probably used in ceremonies and performances; the audiences at such events may well have felt a sense of awe or mystery even if, as many researchers think likely, they knew or guessed that human operators were using mechanisms to make it seem as if the masks were speaking. As for the movable statues, none has yet been found. Other complex mechanisms, however, were designed in various parts of the ancient world. Some of them represented technological developments that would later be used in the first robots.

The Antikythera Mechanism, dating from the second century BCE, was an elaborate calendar-keeping device that tracked the Sun's movement over the course of the year, the phases of the Moon, and lunar and solar eclipses. Made of interlocking gear wheels of various sizes held together by pins and slots, the Antikythera is an early example of clockwork mechanics, a type of mechanical engineering that would appear in some early versions of robots. Another branch of mechanical engineering, pneumatics, deals with compressing air, or forcing it through tubes or pipes, to power machines such as pistons and pumps. (A blowpipe is a simple example of pneumatics in action.) Pneumatics, which was studied in the Mediterranean world as early as the third century BCE, was harnessed to move the limbs of early robots and remains an operating principle of many robots today.

One of the most admired inventors of antiquity was the mathematician and engineer Hero, who was active in the first century BCE. He

ى داخل المسمع مطففة بعض
على بعض و فى دايرها اربعة
عشر عراقها رووسها الجهة
واحد و فى وسط الحلقة صورة
داير الغلاف وبين الحلقة
والغلاف اربع سطيات اطراف
ملصقة بداخل الحلقة ويظاهر
الغلاف وصورة شخص واحد
بيدير ظاهن وموصيعه فى راسها
وره معلقة فكلاب فى اعلى
باب من الابواب الاربعة عشر
وفى اسفلها شظفه باعه موضى
على طرف عراب من الغربان
وعلى الحلقة ض وعلى العيان
و وعلى داير الغلاف ك وع
الشظايا الحامله للحلقة على
الغلاف ب واصل صوره
المسمع و فى داخلها جميع ما كر
قمر الاواصح الحلى يسمى وصعب
الشمعة المقدره وعلها آ
فى علان حمل على قرص ب

**AMONG THE DESIGNS OF THE TWELFTH-CENTURY ARAB ENGINEER AL JAZARI WAS THIS CANDLE CLOCK. THE BURNING OF THE CANDLE FOR AN HOUR CAUSED THE FALCON (ON LEFT) TO DROP A BALL, WHICH OPENED ONE OF THE DOORS AROUND THE BASE, LETTING A MECHANICAL FIGURE EMERGE. THERE IS NO EVIDENCE THAT THIS INGENIOUS CLOCK WAS EVER BUILT.**

must have been one of the busiest inventors of his time, for he is credited with a vast array of designs, including an early version of the steam engine. Hero wrote an influential text on pneumatics; in addition, he experimented with the related field of hydraulics, which is similar to pneumatics except that it exerts pressure on water or some other liquid to drive the action of the machinery. Hero was also known for his work on automata, which are moving, mechanical figures of people and animals. To illustrate some elements of mechanical engineering—such as pulleys, levers, gears, and hydraulic and pneumatic chambers—Hero drew plans for several automata, including singing birds and musicians who played instruments.

No evidence has been found to show that Hero actually constructed any of his automata. Many ancient texts, however, mention such figures. The treasures of kings, for example, were sometimes said to include bejeweled automata. These stories may be the work of imaginative historians who had heard rumors of the automata designed by Hero and other engineers. More than a thousand years after Hero's time, however, his writings were rediscovered, and the idea that the ancients had built such sophisticated constructions inspired engineers and inventors to build their own automata.

During the twelfth century, an Arab-Islamic engineer known as Al Jazari drew designs for a number of devices, including humanoid automata and mechanical clocks and pumps. Around 1495, Italian artist and inventor Leonardo da Vinci drew up plans for a humanoid automaton, a knight that would move its arms and head. Da Vinci is not, however, believed to have built the knight.

One of the earliest confirmed automata was installed in the tower of the cathedral in Strasbourg, France, in 1352. It was a mechanical rooster triggered by the mechanism of a clock. At noon, the rooster flapped its wings and opened its beak, and a pneumatic horn inside it made a crowing sound. Over the next few centuries, clocks with automated figures graced many church towers around Europe. By the sixteenth century, however, some automata were moving about under their own

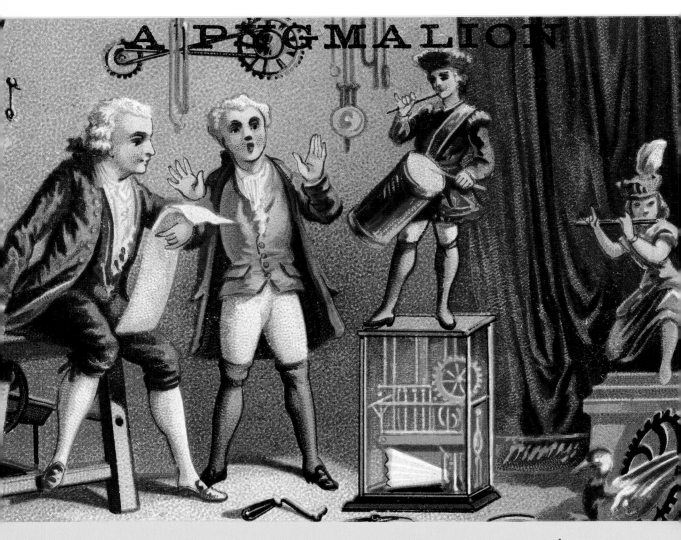

AUDIENCES WERE ASTOUNDED BY THE LIFELIKE MOVEMENTS OF JACQUES DE VAUCANSON'S AUTOMATA, OR MECHANICAL FIGURES. THE FRENCH PHILOSOPHER VOLTAIRE WROTE THAT VAUCANSON "SEEMED TO STEAL THE HEAVENLY FIRES IN HIS SEARCH TO GIVE LIFE."

power, no longer tethered to external clockwork mechanisms.

The Smithsonian Institution in Washington, D.C., houses the wood and iron figure of a monk 15 inches (38 centimeters) high. Like an old-fashioned clock or watch, the monk contains a spring mechanism that is tightened with a key. When this mechanism is activated, a clockwork mechanism inside the monk causes it to pace in a square, bowing its head, moving its lower jaw as though speaking, and raising a rosary to its lips. The history of this skillfully made figure is not fully known, but researchers think that it was constructed in the mid-sixteenth century for Charles V, ruler of the Holy Roman Empire.

During the sixteenth and seventeenth centuries, engineers and jewelers manufactured many automata for the wealthy and powerful of Europe. Some automata, like the walking monk, were operated by clockwork. These were usually fairly small, and some of them moved around independently. They were basically expensive windup toys. A few larger hydraulic or pneumatic automata, attached to fixed bases by their systems of pipes, were incorporated into gardens. In Japan at around the same time, a tradition of mechanical craftsmanship called *karakuri* developed. Artisans and engineers in this tradition made puppets and other devices with clockwork mechanisms, including some free-moving automata. Tea-serving dolls, for example, were knee-high figures that operated on a system of wooden gears and wheels, powered by a spring made of flexible whalebone. The dolls moved back and forth carrying cups of tea on trays.

The stiff, repetitive movements of automata may seem robotic, but these early mechanical people cannot really be considered robots. Their ability to act was limited to whatever set of motions had been built into them from the start. They could not be adapted to other uses—in other words, they could not be reprogrammed. That breakthrough would be made in the eighteenth century by a French engineer named Jacques de Vaucanson. Some historians of technology have called his flute-playing automaton the world's first robot.

Born in 1709, Vaucanson developed an interest in clocks and other mechanisms during his childhood. He came of age at a time when people were debating the differences and similarities between living organisms and machines. In the middle of the previous century, the French philosopher René Descartes argued that animals (and, by extension, people) could be seen as collections of tubes, pumps, and joints—machines that happened to be made out of flesh and bone rather than wood and metal. These speculations inspired new interest in automata. Vaucanson was one of many engineers, physicians, and others who set out to make artificial beings that were more lifelike than any that had been seen before.

In 1738, Vaucanson rented a showroom in Paris. For a fee equal to about a week's wages for an unskilled laborer, he demonstrated the Flute Player, a life-size automaton that, as its name suggested, played the flute. Other musical automata merely moved their hands as though they were playing instruments, while the sounds were produced by mechanical instruments hidden inside the figures. Vaucanson's creation really played the flute. When weighted pulleys acted on bellows inside the automaton, air from the bellows passed up through tubes, out through the figure's mouth, and across the mouthpiece of the flute. The mouth even had a moving metal tongue to vary the amount of air. At the same time, the figure's fingers moved to cover or release the various air holes on the flute.

The elaborate, spring-powered clockwork mechanism that operated the Flute Player's many moving parts was contained in the pedestal on which the automaton stood. The control system for the device was a wooden cylinder with pegs arranged on its surface. Turning a key wound a spring and set the cylinder rotating; the pegs then activated the pulleys, gears, and levers in the proper sequence. What made the Flute Player reprogrammable was that it could play more than one song. Vaucanson created a dozen different cylinders. When the cylinder was changed, the automaton performed a new routine of breathing and fingering, producing a different tune.

Audiences were amazed—or, in some cases, disturbed—by the way the automaton actually breathed. They also noticed that its hands seemed to be clothed in skin; Vaucanson thought the instrument sounded too artificial until he hit on the idea of covering the fingers with fine leather. All in all, the Flute Player seemed very human. In

THE TURK WAS A MECHANICAL CHESS PLAYER THAT WON MOST OF ITS GAMES—IT IS SAID TO HAVE DEFEATED BOTH BENJAMIN FRANKLIN AND NAPOLEON BONAPARTE. THE TURK STIRRED UP CONTROVERSY THAT LASTED FOR YEARS. WAS IT A MARVEL OF ENGINEERING OR A HOAX?

1751 the first volume of a new French encyclopedia included a detailed description of it under the entry *androïde*, from Greek words meaning "like a man." Later this term gave rise to the word *android*.

Vaucanson's show was a big success for more than a year. Then, when attendance began to drop, Vaucanson added two more automata. One was a human figure that played two musical instruments at the same time—a pipe and a tambourine. The other was a duck, perhaps the most lifelike automaton of the era. With more than four hundred moving parts in a single wing, this life-size creation was capable of a wide variety of movement. It dabbled its bill in the water, rose onto its legs, quacked, settled back into a resting position, flapped its wings, and ate pieces of corn that it picked from the surface of the water. It even digested the corn, in a way. Chemicals inside the duck turned the corn into a green material that eventually passed out through the duck's backside.

The eating, pooping duck was Vaucanson's last automaton. Tired of being a showman, the inventor sold his mechanical musicians and his duck. Sadly, they were later lost or destroyed. Although Vaucanson had given up his interest in automata, he remained interested in automation, which is the design and construction of mechanical systems that run themselves. He accepted an appointment from the French government to modernize the nation's silk manufacturing industry.

Focusing on the looms that wove silk into patterns, Vaucanson added mechanisms that made the operation of the loom almost entirely automatic. This increased both the rate of production and the consistency of quality in the finished product. It also threatened to put weavers out of work. In an early example of the anxiety and turmoil that automation would cause across many industries, silk workers went on strike against Vaucanson's proposed reforms in 1744. The king ordered some workers hanged for taking part in the strike, and Vaucanson, attacked in the streets and in fear for his life, had to disguise himself as a monk to escape from the city of Lyon, the center of France's silk industry. The march of automation could not be halted, however. In 1785 an English inventor named Edmund Cartwright

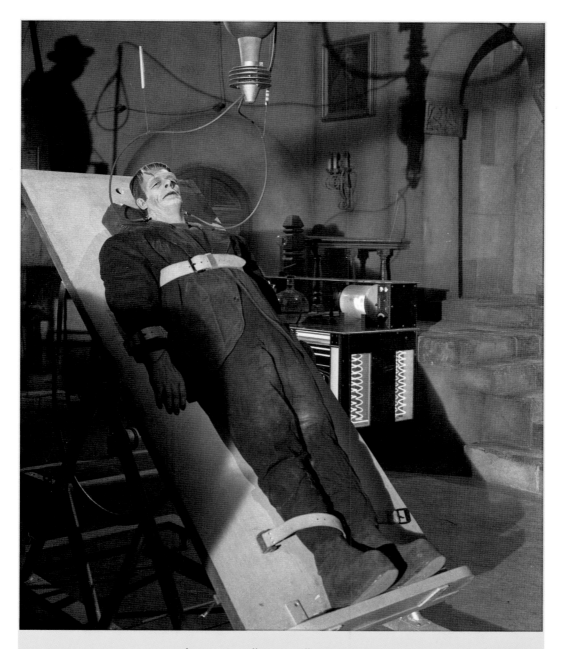

ALTHOUGH FRANKENSTEIN'S FICTIONAL "MONSTER" WAS NOT REALLY A ROBOT, IT RAISED QUESTIONS THAT MAY APPLY TO ROBOTS: IS THE CREATION OF ARTIFICIAL LIFE POSSIBLE? IS IT WISE? WHAT IF WE CANNOT CONTROL OUR CREATIONS?

patented a fully automatic, programmable steam-powered loom that some technology historians regard as the first industrial robot.

While the prospect of automation loomed over industry, jewelers and instrument makers continued to produce impressive, toylike automata. A museum in Neuchâtel, Switzerland, now houses three of the finest surviving examples of their art, built in the late eighteenth century to serve as advertisements for watchmakers. One plays the organ, one draws four different pictures, and one writes with a quill pen and ink. All are operated by mechanisms very similar to Vaucanson's.

Another device built around the same time became one of the most notorious mechanisms of the eighteenth and nineteenth centuries. It was a mechanical chess player constructed in 1769 by a Hungarian engineer named Wolfgang von Kempelen. Made in the form of a Turkish-looking, mustached, turbaned figure sitting at a wooden cupboard with a chessboard on top of it, the device came to be called the Turk.

The Turk had a turbulent history. Although it was a popular sensation when von Kempelen displayed it, he soon took it apart. Later, under pressure from the emperor of Austria-Hungary, von Kempelen reassembled the Turk and took it on a tour of Europe. Everywhere it went, the Turk competed against human chess players, and it usually won. Surely, some people declared, this was the most astonishing mechanical contrivance that had ever been made: a machine that could not just move, but think!

Others were not so sure. A few observers muttered darkly about demonic forces. Most, however, turned their attention to the large chest that supported the chessboard. Although doors in the front of the cabinet were opened before each demonstration, giving the audience a view of the elaborate system of pulleys and gears inside, some speculated that there might be another compartment in the rear of the chest—one big enough to hold a human chess player. Pamphlets arguing that the Turk was a hoax, and others countering that it was genuine, circulated around Europe.

Von Kempelen took the chess player apart before his death in 1804, but in 1818, under new ownership, the Turk was reassembled and went back on the road. In 1826 the supposed automaton came to the United States, where it toured for more than a decade. During this time, the claims of fraud became harder to ignore. Several people claimed to have glimpsed someone crawling out of the machine after demonstrations, and in 1834 a French magazine published a "confession" by one of the men who had operated the Turk from inside. The truth gradually came out. Over the years, a number of chess players had occupied the Turk, moving the game pieces with a mechanical arm (and winning most of their matches). The Turk, in short, was no Deep Blue. But even though von Kempelen had not created a "thinking machine," the mechanical arm he had given to his creation was so well designed that it would later influence the makers of robotic arms.

Hoax though it was, von Kempelen's automated chess player had entertained thousands of people. Other entertainments of the period dealt with the act of creating a replica of a human being. In Mary Shelley's 1818 novel *Frankenstein,* a doctor builds a man out of stolen body parts and then imbues his creation with life—only to be destroyed by the creature, which proves to have an all-too-human desire for revenge, as well as the gentler qualities of affection and curiosity. Although Frankenstein's "monster" was not really a robot, Shelley's theme of the creator who is unable to control his creation runs through many later stories about robots. At the same time, with the Industrial Revolution under way, people were growing increasingly accustomed to automation and mechanization. In the late nineteenth century, as a stream of labor-saving devices and other marvels flowed from the workshops of inventors, the mechanical human gained new life in both fiction and fact.

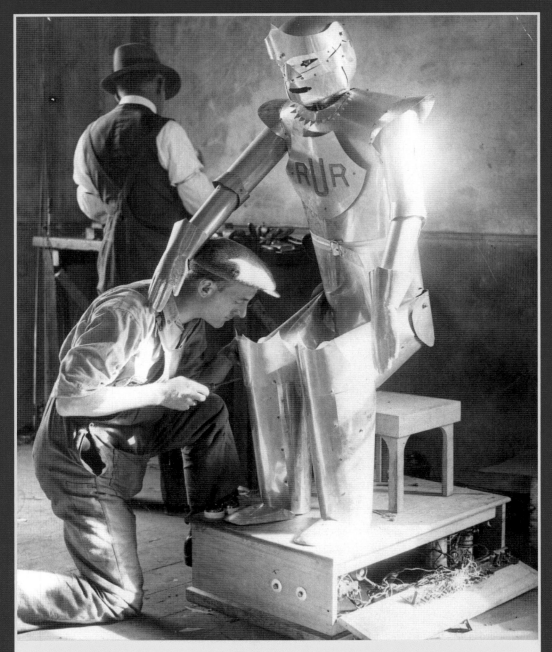

As robots moved from fiction to reality, some early experimenters tried to build humanoid "mechanical men." Real strides in robot science, though, came when inventors focused not on how a robot looked but on what it could do.

# First Steps

In 1865 Edward S. Ellis, the author of countless nineteenth-century American pulp novels, published *The Huge Hunter, or The Steam Man of the Prairies.* In this book, a brilliant teenage inventor and his friends travel around in a wagon pulled by a giant mechanical man. The huge cart-puller was not really a robot, but a moving engine that operated on the same principles as a steam locomotive. Ellis never explained why its inventor had given it the form of a walking man instead of a running horse or, for that matter, a carriage. The idea of an immense humanoid figure stalking the landscape must have had a certain appeal, however. The Steam Man of the Prairies strode on through a string of sequels, although electricity eventually replaced steam as its source of power.

A few decades after the Steam Man made his appearance in fiction, one of the era's greatest inventors created a splash with a different kind of robot in a specially built indoor pond in New York City's Madison Square Garden. Nikola Tesla, a Serbian who had immigrated to the United States, had won his place in the history of technology by developing the alternating-current system of electricity and designing a hydroelectric power plant at Niagara Falls. Tesla was also the inventor of radio, although for many years the credit for this invention was given to the Italian inventor Guglielmo Marconi.

During the latter part of Tesla's career, one of his chief interests was transmitting energy without wires. In 1898 he patented an invention that he called "Method of and Apparatus for Controlling Mechanism of Moving Vessels or Vehicles." Hoping to arouse interest among potential customers or investors, Tesla entered the device in a show of new electrical equipment at Madison Square Garden. The moving vessel he chose to operate was a small, iron-hulled boat.

"When first shown . . . it created a sensation such as no other invention of mine has ever produced," Tesla later wrote of his remote-controlled boat. Never before had a machine been moved about from a distance, without wires or cables. Tesla's boat did not move through a preprogrammed sequence of actions, like the praying monk or Vaucanson's Flute Player—at any moment, Tesla could turn the boat this way or that on the pond.

The boat moved through the water by the action of a motor-driven propeller, and it changed direction with a motor-driven rudder. Batteries inside the boat provided power to the motors. Standing some distance away from the tank, Tesla governed the operation of the rudder and propeller, as well as lights on the bow and stern of the boat, through his remote-control device, which emitted radio signals. The signals were picked up by coherers, or radio-activated switches, on a panel in the boat. These coherers contained magnetic metallic powders that aligned themselves with the electromagnetic pulses of the radio waves. Once Tesla's signal had aligned the powders, the coherers conducted electrical current through the boat's wiring, operating the levers, gears, and springs that controlled the action of the propeller, rudder, and lights.

Although Tesla made operating the boat look easy, the control system was more complex than it looked. Tesla not only had to invent the coherers but also had to work out mechanisms for translating electrical impulses into specific tasks, such as turning the rudder to the right. Constructing the first remote control was a technological triumph and an early milestone in the history of what would later be called robotics.

Tesla called the boat a teleautomaton. Today it would be called a telerobot. It is a direct ancestor of the remote-controlled submersibles that explorers send to probe the secrets of shipwrecks and undersea caves, and of the robotic vehicles that NASA's scientists steer across the red plains of Mars.

Tesla envisioned a host of possible uses for his remote-control technology. The U.S. Navy, he thought, might use his radio control system to guide torpedoes directly at enemy ships or harbors. So might other navies—author Mark Twain wrote to his friend Tesla, offering to represent the inventor in the sale of the "destructive terror which you have been inventing" to England and Germany. No one, however, was interested in radio-controlled devices, even in an age that was getting used to inventions such as the telephone and the moving picture. Finally, in 1916, the U.S. Navy financed some experiments with the technology, but by that time Tesla's patent on it had expired. Tesla never made any money from his invention of radio-controlled telerobotics.

The future of robots was shaped in part by an industrial development that occurred early in the twentieth century. In 1913, American automobile manufacturer Henry Ford introduced the conveyor-belt assembly line to his factory. Manufacturers had already streamlined factory work by breaking processes into steps and having each worker perform just one or two of the steps. Instead of assembling a chair, for example, a worker now spent the whole day attaching chair legs to seats, then handing the partly built chair on to other workers who would add the backs, seat covers, and other parts. Ford's plant, however, was the first to move the product being assembled through the factory on a conveyor belt. This meant that workers could stand in one place and perform their tasks again and again without wasting time by moving around.

Ford boasted that the new system allowed workers to build a Model T car from the ground up in just ninety-three minutes, and soon the assembly-line system was adopted in many other manufacturing operations. With factory workers remaining stationary and performing repetitive tasks, the stage was set for industrial robots. Such robots

HENRY FORD DEVELOPED THE ASSEMBLY LINE TO IMPROVE THE EFFICIENCY OF HIS AUTOMOBILE MANUFACTURING OPERATION. IN DOING SO, HE CREATED THE IDEAL SETTING FOR THE INDUSTRIAL ROBOT.

would not have to move around—all that would be required of them was to perform a task repeatedly and accurately. And they would not have to resemble human beings. An arm alone would do the job.

In 1934 an engineer named Willard Pollard Jr. filed a patent application for an industrial robot. It was an automatic spray-painting device that consisted of an electrical control system and a mechanical arm. The control system was activated by a strip of film with holes punched in it; the speed of the motors varied according to how close together or far apart the holes were. The arm itself was a version of a centuries-old instrument called a pantograph. Originally invented to allow people to make multiple copies of written texts or drawings, pantographs are arrangements of bars fastened together by joints that keep the bars in fixed relationships to each other as they move. With a pantographic writing device, for example, when a person writes something with a pen attached to the end of one bar, a pen on the other bar duplicates the movements of the first pen.

Von Kempelen's fraudulent chess-playing automaton had contained a pantograph. The machine's game was played by an operator hiding inside the mechanism. When the operator used a pantographic arm to move a piece on a board inside the secret compartment, the other part of the mechanism, disguised as the Turk's arm, manipulated the piece on the chessboard above. Pollard's robot arm worked in a similar fashion. The motors controlled the movement of one end, causing the other end, which was fitted with the paint sprayer, to execute the same movements. The system could move the arm in five directions; today, roboticists would say that the arm had five degrees of freedom.

The first thing that set this industrial robot apart from other kinds of automated factory equipment, such as looms, was its range of motion. The second was the fact that it could be reprogrammed to paint in different patterns by changing the film strip. Beyond that, the arm could be adapted to manipulate other tools, not just paint sprayers. In the early 1940s, the DeVilbiss paint company built a prototype, or first model, of Pollard's arm, as well as a prototype of a similar instrument

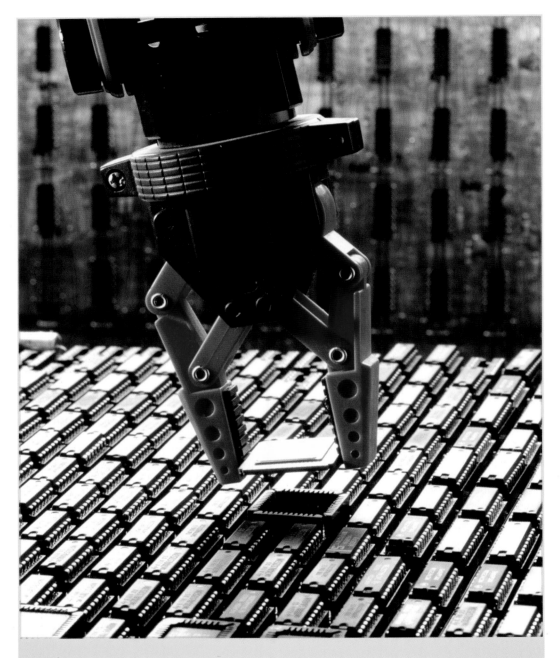

A ROBOT ARM MANIPULATING MICROPROCESSOR CHIPS IS A MODERN DESCENDANT OF THE FIRST INDUSTRIAL ROBOT, DESIGNED IN THE 1930S TO PERFORM AUTOMATIC SPRAY-PAINTING.

invented by Harold Roselund. The robot arms worked, but they did not attract much interest, and they were never manufactured on a commercial basis. Not for another twenty years would robots start to make their first advances onto the factory floor. By that time, new electronic technology had made strips of punched film obsolete. They were replaced by a new control system: the computer.

Computers are machines that store information and instructions. The key to a computer's operation is the switch, an electricity-conducting device that is either open or closed at all times. Tesla's coherer was an early form of a switch. So was the vacuum tube, a small glass container from which air had been removed. Electrons in the tube, moving in response to electrical impulses, shifted the tube between open and closed states. In the late 1940s, three American scientists working at Bell Laboratories invented a new type of switch called the transistor. Compared with the vacuum-filled tube, the transistor was small, energy-efficient, and solid. The transistor also operated much more quickly than the vacuum tube. It launched the field known as solid-state electronics, the design and manufacture of electronic equipment containing transistors.

By the time the transistor was invented, the first digital computers had already been built. These room-sized machines used vacuum tubes as switches. ENIAC—the first large-scale, electronic, digital, programmable computer—was built at the University of Pennsylvania for the U.S. Army, and put into use in 1947. It contained 17,468 vacuum tubes and could perform 5,000 simple addition or subtraction calculations each second, or 385 calculations involving multiplication. By the 1960s, transistors had replaced vacuum tubes in computers, greatly increasing their speed, compactness, and computing power. The next advance in switch technology was the integrated circuit, also called a microchip or microprocessor, which packed many microscopically small transistors onto a small wafer. (Microprocessors today have millions of transistors on wafers smaller than your little fingernail.) During the 1970s, microprocessors powered another enormous leap forward in computing technology. They made personal computers and computerized appliances possible. They also brought about a revolution in robot making.

Robots had not advanced very far during the first part of the twentieth century. Around midcentury, however, scientists and engineers started introducing new ideas and machines, and the era of modern robots began.

One of the best-known robots of the time was Elektro, manufactured by the Westinghouse Corporation for the 1939 World's Fair in New York City. Elektro was a 7-foot-tall (2-meter-tall) humanoid robot, a steel skeleton covered by gleaming aluminum. It could glide on its wheeled feet, turn its head, and—as many people did in those days—smoke cigarettes. It contained a record player to simulate speech. Eventually joined by Sparko, a barking robot dog, Elektro greeted visitors to the Westinghouse exhibit at the fair with utterances such as "My brain is bigger than yours." Neither Elektro nor Sparko could wander far, however. Both were teleautomata, controlled by operators who were located close at hand. Electrical cables attached discreetly to the robots' feet carried the operators' instructions. Elektro and Sparko were handsomely designed and cleverly built, but they did not represent any real advance in robot design.

Still, when most people of the time thought of robots, they pictured Elektro, or something like it—a manlike metal being, often bigger than a human, and usually without the cigarette. This popular concept of the robot, however, had little in common with the next steps toward genuine robots. Those next steps did not look at all like Elektro, or even Sparko. A couple of them, however, did look a little like tortoises.

The tortoise robot was the work of a British-American scientist and inventor named William Grey Walter. As a neurophysiologist, Walter studied the structure and function of the brain. He made a number of significant contributions to brain science, including improving the design of the electroencephalograph (a machine that records brain waves) and using it to locate tumors or other damage in the brain. Walter was

ELEKTRO, ONE OF EIGHT ROBOTS BUILT BY WESTINGHOUSE IN THE 1930S, ENTERTAINED AUDIENCES WITH SUCH FEATS AS CONDUCTING MUSIC AND EVEN SMOKING CIGARETTES. HERE HE IS CONDUCTING CELLIST LOIS KENDALL AT THE WORLD'S FAIR IN 1939. THE ROBOT DID NOT MOVE INDEPENDENTLY, HOWEVER. IT WAS A TELEROBOT, CONTROLLED BY A REMOTE OPERATOR.

also interested in how the brain works. His theory was that brainpower has more to do with the connections, or "wiring," between brain cells than with the number of cells. To test the idea that complex behavior could arise from a small number of brain cells, Walter built a pair of simple battery-powered robots in 1948 and 1949. He called them Elmer and Elsie and liked to say that their species name was *Machina speculatrix,* Latin for "the machine that watches."

*M. speculatrix* was a plastic shell mounted on three wheels. The front wheel was attached to two small motors, one to propel the robot forward and the other to turn it. The robot's brain was extremely simple. It consisted of two vacuum tubes and two sensors, one for light and one for pressure. The light sensor was connected to the front wheel. When this sensor registered light, it steered the robot in that direction. The second sensor was mounted on the shell. When this sensor registered pressure—meaning that the robot had bumped into something— it halted the robot. The way these small, shelled beings moved slowly across the floor led people to call them "Walter's tortoises."

The tortoises confirmed Walter's belief that just a few simple, wired-in reactions—in this case, the reflexes of moving toward light and halting at pressure—could produce complex-seeming behavior. People who observed the tortoises could not escape the impression that the little robots were actively exploring their environment and figuring out how to get around obstacles. Walter once attached a light to the top of one of the tortoises and then placed a mirror in front of it. The tortoise kept trying to move toward the light reflected in the mirror. Each time, however, it bumped into the mirror and stopped. Walter described its motions as "flickering" and "jigging." If the same activity were seen in an animal, he said, it "might be accepted as evidence of some degree of self-awareness."

Walter's tortoises marked an important point in robot history. They were the first autonomous, or self-directing, robots. Unlike Elektro, the tortoises were not under the direct control of an operator, nor did they move according to a predetermined program. The tortoises "decided" where to go based on stimuli from the world around them. Although mainstream robot science after the mid-twentieth century focused on machines with more complex, digital-computer brains, the simple structure of Walter's tortoises would later inspire some researchers to seek an alternative approach to robot design.

The 1950s brought new kinds of remote-controlled and programmed robots, laying the groundwork for many later developments. One influential invention was the "master-slave" robotic arm completed in 1951 by Raymond Goertz. Created to handle dangerous radioactive material, the arm was a telerobot, manipulated by a human operator who was some distance away, safely shielded from the radiation. The "slave" part of the machine mimicked the movements of the "master."

The next breakthrough was made by George C. Devol, who had observed that a great deal of work involved people picking things up and moving them from one place to another. A machine could do that, Devol thought. In 1954 he applied for a patent for a general-purpose, solid-state electronic industrial robot that could be programmed in a wide variety of ways to "transfer articles"—in other words, to move or carry stuff. Two years later, in partnership with an engineer named Joseph Engelberger and with financial backing from the Consolidated Diesel Electronic Company, Devol founded a company called Unimation (short for "universal automation"). He and Engelberger began marketing the Unimate, as they called their industrial robot.

In 1961 the first Unimate was installed in a General Motors plant in Trenton, New Jersey. The job it performed—handling freshly made, red-hot metal parts such as door handles—was so dangerous and unpleasant that few of the plant's three thousand human workers were willing to perform it. For this reason, the workers did not object to having a robot join their assembly line. As Engelberger later said, "It helped with working people that the first robots were put to work doing hot, hazardous, and dull labor."

Engelberger and Devol had hoped that other factories across the United States would clamor for robots, but that didn't happen. Europe

ORIGINALLY DEVELOPED FOR HANDLING RADIOACTIVE MATERIAL, THESE AMERICAN-BUILT
REMOTELY OPERATED MECHANICAL HANDS WERE SENSITIVE ENOUGH TO PIN A DIAPER ON A
DOLL, AS DEMONSTRATED AT A GERMAN INDUSTRIAL FAIR IN 1954.

and Japan, however, showed considerable interest; Japan was especially willing to embrace the idea of industrial robots. In 1968 Unimation licensed its robot technology to Kawasaki Heavy Industries of Japan, kicking off a burst of Japanese robot research and development. By the 1980s Japan had become the world leader in robot use. Many historians of modern industry say that Japan's early adoption of industrial robots was a key factor in making the country a leader in the manufacture of high-quality consumer goods such as automobiles and electronic devices.

An anecdote told by Joseph Engelberger illustrates the different attitudes toward robots that prevailed in United States and Japan at the end of the 1960s. Engelberger appeared on a late-night television show with the prototype of a programmable humanoid robot. Unlike Unimate, this machine matched the popular image of a robot, and the show's producers had asked for it to be programmed to do a beer commercial. The demonstration was a huge hit with the audience. "But after that," Engelberger said, "the only calls I got were from people who wanted my robot to be entertainment at the county fair." Soon Engelberger went to Japan at the invitation of a trade group. There he met with five hundred business executives who had gathered to learn about practical ways of using robots in industry. In the United States, it would be some time before robots truly moved beyond the realm of entertainment. Today, however, Engelberger is widely recognized around the world as the father of the modern robotics industry. Each year since 1977, a highly respected prize called the Engelberger Award has gone to the individual who has done the most to further "the science of robotics in the service of mankind."

COG IS A HUMANOID ROBOT BUILT TO TEST THE THEORY THAT WE GAIN INTELLIGENCE BY INTERACTING WITH PEOPLE AND THE WORLD. IT IS ONE OF SEVERAL PROJECTS AT THE MASSACHUSETTS INSTITUTE OF TECHNOLOGY'S ARTIFICIAL INTELLIGENCE LAB.

# Robotics and Artificial Intelligence

The year 1907 saw the publication of *Ozma of Oz,* with its likable character Tiktok. That same year, a movie called *The Mechanical Statue and the Ingenious Servant* was released. It told a foreboding, Frankensteinian tale about a powerful automaton that went out of control, became dangerous, and had to be destroyed by its creator. Grim warnings about machines echoed in other movies, too. Charlie Chaplin's 1936 film *Modern Times* showed humans cast out of work and into misery by automated factories. Five years later, *Man Made Monster* told of a scientist (a mad one, naturally) who used electronic equipment to seize control of a man and operate him like a robot.

Movies were not the only place where robots ran amok. There were even more mechanical monsters in the pulp science-fiction magazines of the day, such as *Amazing Stories,* founded in 1926. But not all of the fictional robots of the era were evil. Lester del Rey's 1938 story "Helen O'Loy" is about an android woman who falls in love with, and marries, her creator. The following year, the brothers Earl and Otto Binder, under the name Eando Binder, began publishing a series of stories about Adam Link. This android's heroic qualities are conveyed by such titles as "Adam Link, Champion Athlete," "Adam Link, Robot Detective," and "Adam Link Saves the World."

Isaac Asimov was in his late teens when "Helen O'Loy" and the first Adam Link story appeared. By that time Asimov had been reading science fiction for years. He knew that del Rey and the Binder brothers were unusual in their positive treatment of robots. The young Asimov had grown weary of what he later called "the ever-repeated robot plot" involving "hordes of clanking, murderous robots." He said, "I didn't see robots that way. I saw them as machines. . . . They might be dangerous but surely safety factors would be built in." At the age of nineteen, Asimov started writing his own stories about robots, showing how they might operate within the boundaries of those safety factors.

Asimov's third robot story, "Liar!", was published in *Astounding Science Fiction* in May 1941. It contained a reference to something called the First Law of Robotics. The following March, Asimov expanded on this idea, inventing the Three Laws of Robotics in the story "Runaround." The three laws were:

1. A robot may not injure a human being or, through inaction, allow a human being to come to harm.
2. A robot must obey the orders given to it by a human being except where such orders would conflict with the First Law.
3. A robot must protect its own existence as long as such protection does not conflict with the First or Second Laws.

The hero of "Runaround" is a robot known as SPD-13, called Speedy by its human operators, who are stranded on the broiling planet Mercury. To get Speedy to provide the help they need, they must find a way to resolve a situation that the robot sees as a conflict between the Second and Third Laws. Asimov went on to write a number of stories and novels about robots, almost all of them incorporating the Three Laws. The stories generally explore situations in which a robot, for some reason, cannot apply the Three Laws straightforwardly; many of the tales take the form of mysteries. (The 2004 movie *I, Robot*, which borrowed the title of a collection of Asimov's stories, featured a robot suspected of being a murderer. It was advertised with the Three Laws, followed by the ominous phrase "Rules were made to be broken.")

THE CRIME-SOLVING, WORLD-SAVING HERO OF EANDO BINDER'S STORIES WAS A ROBOT NAMED ADAM LINK, ONE OF THE FEW POSITIVE PORTRAYALS OF ROBOTS IN EARLY SCIENCE FICTION. ("I, ROBOT," THE TITLE OF A BINDER STORY, WAS LATER GIVEN TO A COLLECTION OF ROBOT STORIES BY ISAAC ASIMOV.)

Speedy had a "positronic brain," like all of Asimov's robots. The phrase has no real meaning, but it suggests some kind of supercomputer using positrons, which are subatomic particles. Since Asimov's time, other science-fiction writers have adopted the handy positronic brain as a way of accounting for the advanced, humanlike thinking abilities of their robots and androids. Many of them have also adopted the Three Laws of Robotics, to which Asimov later added a fourth (he called it the Zeroth Law because he wanted it to come before the First Law in the list). It read: "A robot may not harm humanity or, by inaction, allow humanity to come to harm." This added law makes robots responsible for protecting the entire human race, not just individuals.

"Runaround" introduced more than the Three Laws. It also introduced the word *robotics*, which Asimov had coined. The study, design, and creation of robots now had a name. But although Asimov had added a new dimension of thoughtfulness and seriousness to robot fiction, the robots of the real world were very far from having the mental capacity to grasp the Three Laws, much less be stymied by them. In the 1960s, however, robots did advance on one important front. They started to walk.

The Unimate proved that a robot arm could function efficiently. What about robot legs? The designers who set out to build robots with legs soon learned that it was one thing to create a functioning leg and quite another to make it walk. On its own, a mechanical leg could operate much like a mechanical arm—but a leg does not usually operate on its own. Together with one or more other legs, it walks.

In humans and animals, walking calls upon a sense called proprioception, or body awareness. This is the sense of where one's body is in space, how it is oriented, and how its various limbs are moving relative to one another. Proprioception is what keeps us from falling over when we lift one foot off the ground. During walking, proprioception involves many minute adjustments of balance as we swing one leg forward, plant that foot, shift our weight, push off from the other leg, then swing that leg forward, shifting our weight again, and repeat. Proprioception and

Isaac Asimov, author of many stories about robots, coined the term *ROBOTICS* and invented the Three Laws, which are meant to keep robots from harming humans.

walking must be learned, as anyone knows who has ever watched a young child learn to sit, then to crawl, and finally to take his or her first unsteady steps.

Edward Ellis, creator of the fictional Steam Man of the Prairies, may not have realized how difficult it would be to make a walking robot. In the 1960s, a General Electric (GE) engineer named Ralph Mosher grappled with the problem. Working on a contract for the U.S. Defense Department, Mosher created a truck with four legs instead of wheels. It was not a true robot, because it was operated by a driver, but the computer-controlled electronics that regulated the movements of the four legs were no different from those that would be found in a robot. GE's walking truck, which looked a bit like a jeep mounted on four tall jointed legs, had a top speed of about 4 miles (6.4 kilometers) an hour, comparable to a human pace. Designed as a tool to carry soldiers' equipment over rough terrain, the truck could climb over or maneuver around obstacles. Some sources say that photographs of the walking truck were one of the inspirations for the giant walkers that attacked the rebel base in the Star Wars film *The Empire Strikes Back*.

While GE was developing the walking truck, another research center took a different approach to robotic locomotion. The Stanford Research Institute in California (now called the SRI Artificial Intelligence Center) developed a landmark robot called Shakey, which was introduced to the public in 1968.

Shakey was about knee-high and consisted of a videocamera sitting on top of a square computer that was mounted on a platform with motorized wheels. The robot could turn in all directions. It was equipped with wires called bump sensors that stuck out of its platform like whiskers, enabling it to feel objects in its path and all around it.

What made Shakey revolutionary was the computer—Shakey was the first computer-controlled mobile robot. Its programming allowed it to perceive its environment through the videocamera, the bump sensors, and an instrument called a triangulating range finder, which measured the distances to objects in the environment. Analyzing this data

ROBOTS IN THE SCIENCE MUSEUM IN LONDON, ENGLAND, USE ULTRASONIC SENSORS TO DETECT OBJECTS AROUND THEM; THEY COMMUNICATE WITH EACH OTHER THROUGH INFRARED SIGNALS. OPERATORS USING JOYSTICKS CAN MAKE THE ROBOTS CHASE EACH OTHER OR DANCE TOGETHER.

required more computing power than Shakey could carry around, so the robot used radio signals to link with a large computer in another room. That computer was part of Shakey's brain; it just happened to be physically separate. Using information gathered from its sensors, Shakey created a "map" of its environment—a room—and used that map to navigate around. The robot could also use the information it had collected to plan new actions, such as executing a command to push a box from one side of the room to another.

SRI called Shakey "the first mobile robot to reason about its actions." Roboticists now regard Shakey as the first robot to have artificial intelligence, or AI, although it was a very basic form of AI.

Artificial intelligence, as a concept and a field of study, was an outgrowth of the development of computers. At first, computers seemed like little more than superpowerful calculators, but it soon became clear that they were capable of much more. As programming became more sophisticated in the late 1940s and the 1950s, people began to wonder how smart these "smart machines" would become. Could a computer ever be made to think? If a computer *could* think, then so could a robot.

In 1950 British mathematician and cryptographer Alan Turing, one of the founders of computer science, published a paper titled "Computing Machinery and Intelligence." Turing was tired of being asked, "Can machines think?" He considered the question meaningless because it did not specify what was meant by "thinking" (a question that philosophers and scientists still cannot answer definitively). Instead, Turing referred to a party game that was popular at the time, in which a man and a woman, in separate rooms, provided typewritten answers to questions from the party guests. The man tried to make the guests think he was the woman, and vice versa. The point of the game was to see how different or similar men's and women's thinking processes were, and whether one gender could successfully pretend to be the other, using only the written word.

What if, Turing asked, one of the hidden subjects were a machine? Would a human questioner be able to tell the difference between answers written by a person and answers written by a machine? If not, Turing proposed, then the machine was entitled to be called intelligent. Turing's proposal has come to be called the "Turing test" for evaluating machine intelligence.

By the year 2000, Turing predicted, properly programmed computers would be able to fool 30 percent of questioners in five-minute Turing tests. That did not happen. Although there have been some cases in which people have thought that computer conversation programs they encountered online were real people, none of these cases has met the standards of the Turing test. The Loebner Prize was established in 1990 to reward the maker of the first conversational computer program (sometimes called a chatterbot) that can pass the Turing test. In the annual competition for the prize, the questioner faces two computer screens. One is activated by a human in another room. The other is activated by a chatterbot. As of early 2007, no chatterbot had managed to fool a questioner, although smaller prizes are awarded each year for the most humanlike program.

Will a computer ever pass the Turing test? Inventor Ray Kurzweil thinks that it will happen by 2029. Some researchers, however, have questioned whether the Turing test is meaningful. In fact, Turing's 1950 paper suggested several versions of the test. The differences among these versions, as well as various objections to the test and responses to the objections, have formed the subject of long, complex debates among roboticists, computer scientists, and philosophers.

One common objection to the usefulness of the Turing test is that even if a computer learned to simulate, or imitate, human thought patterns well enough to fool someone, that would not necessarily mean that it was truly intelligent. What about the ability to write a poem or compose a symphony? In response, some people have pointed out that most people don't write poems or compose symphonies. In any case, researchers have created programs that allow computers to write poems and music in laboratory studies, and to paint as well.

The Turing test provided an initial focus for the study of machine

ENGINEER AND INVENTOR RALPH MOSHER, SEATED IN THE COCKPIT, PUTS HIS WALKING
MACHINE THROUGH ITS PACES. MECHANICAL WALKING POSES COMPLEX CHALLENGES TO
ROBOT DESIGNERS.

thought, a field that grew rapidly after 1956. That year, Dartmouth College in Vermont hosted a two-month meeting called the Artificial Intelligence (AI) Conference. Under the leadership of pioneering researchers such as Marvin Minsky, a cofounder of the AI Laboratory at the Massachusetts Institute of Technology (MIT), AI became a wide-ranging field of study and experimentation during the second half of the twentieth century. Although discussions of the Turing test continue, much of today's serious AI research is focused not on attempts to pass the test but on other approaches to machine thought. Researchers are investigating the nature of intelligence, the processes by which we learn, and ways to improve computer programs and robots.

Scientists learn more about the human brain and nervous system every day. They still do not know, however, how people think—how memories are organized, how thoughts are formed, or how information combines in new ways to form ideas. In trying to meet the challenge of replicating some of the still-mysterious operations of the human brain, AI researchers have taken two general approaches to machine intelligence. Turing and others have called these the top-down and bottom-up approaches.

The top-down approach to AI starts from the idea that human cognition, or thinking, is much like an extremely sophisticated software program. Creating AI will be a matter of first figuring out that program and then writing a similar one that can be installed in computers and robots.

Attempts to create a conversation program that can pass the Turing test are examples of top-down AI. Another example is the Cyc Project, an AI project aimed at creating a computerized knowledge base that will give artificial intelligences a very human kind of thoughtfulness: the practical knowledge that is often called common sense. Doug Lenat, who founded the Cyc Project in 1984, realized that cognition is more than just facts. It requires an understanding of how facts are related to each other, and also of universal realities, such as "unsupported things fall down." Common sense also includes logic, the rules

IN THE 2004 MOVIE *I, ROBOT*, A HUMANOID ROBOT NAMED SONNY THREATENS HUMAN SURVIVAL.

that allow statements to be combined to yield new information or to answer questions. As an example, Lenat cites the statements "All trees are plants" and "All plants eventually die." A computer that has acquired these two pieces of information is capable of answering the question, "Will this tree die?"

Lenat began the Cyc Project (the name Cyc is short for "Encyclopedia") by reading randomly chosen passages from books and then listing all of the assumptions each passage contained—the underlying pieces of knowledge that the author assumed every reader would possess, such as the difference between turkey the bird and Turkey the country. Lenat has been feeding those pieces of knowledge into Cyc ever since, aided by a corps of researchers that now includes volunteers around the world who participate through the Internet.

Cyc's knowledge base is still growing, but many related projects focus on *using* the knowledge base in various types of AI applications. Lenat's company carried out one such project for the U.S. Defense Department. After Cyc was fed a mass of information about past terrorist attacks and techniques, the program was asked to predict possible future terrorist activity. Cyc had some successes, such as predicting that the disease anthrax could be sent through the mail; six months later, in the fall of 2001, this happened. Other predictions were less useful, as when Cyc suggested that Al-Qaeda might send a thousand bomb-wearing dolphins to attack the Hoover Dam. Each success or failure gives project managers an opportunity to feed more knowledge into Cyc, which can also learn by asking questions.

Early in the project, Cyc asked, "Am I human?" Cyc also wanted to know if computers are human. These questions seem to suggest a desire for self-knowledge, which is a very human quality; the questions appear personal, however, in structure they are no different from other inquiries related to organizing knowledge, such as "Is an oak a tree?" or "Are cats animals?" No matter how much knowledge Cyc acquires, it is unlikely to develop a sense of self, but the commonsense knowledge base may prove vital to the future development of AI in both computers and robots.

The bottom-up approach to artificial intelligence is different. It start from the notion that cognition grows gradually out of interconnections among neurons in the human brain, as the brain is used, rather than coming from a high-level organizing system. The Cog project has approached the acquisition of knowledge about the world this way, from the bottom up. Cog—the name is a pun on "cognition" and the cogs, or teeth, of a mechanical gear—is the brainchild of Rodney Brooks of MIT's Artificial Intelligence Laboratory. Using the theory that humans acquire intelligence by interacting with the world, Brooks designed Cog to interact with people and with its environment in the way that a

KISMET, SHOWN HERE WITH ITS CREATOR, CYNTHIA BREAZEAL, IS A "ROBOT BABY" THAT RESPONDS TO ITS ENVIRONMENT MUCH AS A HUMAN BABY DOES. IT APPEARS SAD WHEN IT IS IGNORED, HAPPY WHEN IT IS PLAYED WITH, AND AGITATED WHEN IT IS OVER-STIMULATED.

young human does, such as by following people's movements with its eyes (cameras) and mimicking their movements. Cog is a humanoid robot, a torso with a head, eyes, trunk, and arms that are equipped with proprioception and capable of a wide range of movement. The robot's humanoid form, for which a face is now being developed, encourages people to interact with the robot as though it were human. Cog has not yet been equipped with long-term memory; it is less a computer than a tool for studying how human–robot interaction can shape a robot's development. When asked whether Cog can pass the Turing test, the project's researchers reply, "No . . . but then again, neither could an infant."

The MIT lab also contains a kind of robot baby. Created by Cynthia Breazeal, head of the lab's Sociable Machines Project, Kismet is a mechanical head with movable eyes, eyebrows, ears, and a mouth on a movable jaw. It can turn and tilt its head. Designed to be expressive, Kismet is programmed to behave much like a human infant. It sees and hears social cues from its environment, then responds with social signals of its own. If someone or something approaches the robot too closely, Kismet draws back its head, but if someone speaks from a distance, Kismet leans forward as if to hear better. The robot also smiles and babbles. Researchers think that the study of Kismet's interactions with the world may offer insights into how babies learn to be sociable. Kismet is also yielding ideas about how to make humanoid robots seem more sociable, and thus, safe and acceptable as caretakers and companions. In the future, human-robot interaction may be a fact of everyday life. Perhaps Kismet is leading the way.

Science-fiction stories and movies, such as the 2001 film *A.I.*, usually present artificial intelligence as the capacity to think as well as—or better than—a human being. If general-purpose androids and robots are ever to become a reality, they may require some version of comprehensive, humanlike AI. For the present, however, many robotics researchers tend to focus on smaller-scale goals. Instead of trying to make a robot that thinks like a person, they want to make robots that are good at just a few specific things.

In the early 1970s, just a few years after Unimate went to work in the automobile factory and the GE walking truck and Shakey were unveiled, a research team at Waseda University in Tokyo, Japan, started building the world's first humanoid robot. Led by Ichiro Kato, the team created WABOT-1. This robot could walk, although it moved very slowly, and it could pick up objects with its hands. It could also carry on a limited conversation, offering prerecorded replies to specific statements or questions. At the time, WABOT-1's creators likened its intelligence to that of an eighteen-month-old child. Some observers have called that a generous assessment. Yet WABOT-1 was a landmark robot, not just because it was the first humanoid robot but because it marked Japan's emergence as a leader in robotics.

The Japanese-owned Honda Motor Company took the next big step in humanoid robotics—literally—when it began a project to build a humanoid robot for general household and entertainment use. Honda started with walking. In 1986 the company exhibited an experimental model called E0, which was just a set of computer-controlled legs. Capable of taking a step in five seconds, E0 was an improvement on WABOT-1, which had required about forty-five seconds to complete each step.

By model E3, unveiled in 1987, Honda had achieved robot legs with an effective walking gait. The experimental models that followed gained the ability to climb stairs. They also acquired a body, head, and arms. In 1993 Honda displayed P1, its first prototype of a humanoid robot. This creation was sturdy, even somewhat imposing—it was 6 feet 2 inches (188 centimeters) tall and weighed 386 pounds (175 kilograms). Four years later, P3 was considerably smaller and lighter. Like the earlier models, it was a telerobot, powered by electrical cables and driven by a human operator using a remote control.

In 2000 Honda released the first model that was not considered an experiment or prototype. It was called ASIMO, usually explained as standing for "Advanced Step in Innovative Mobility," although many people have noticed that the name closely resembles that of Isaac Asimov, the

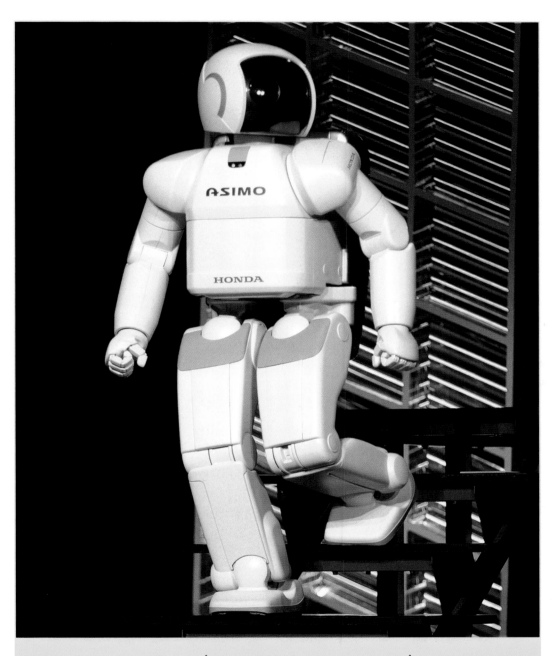

THE HONDA MOTOR COMPANY'S NIMBLE **ASIMO** IS ONE OF THE WORLD'S MOST ADVANCED ROBOTS WHERE PHYSICAL MOBILITY IS CONCERNED, BUT IT LACKS THE ABILITY TO ACT INDEPENDENTLY.

author of many science-fiction stories about robots. ASIMO was smaller and lighter than the prototypes and carried its own supply of battery power. Its silver-white metallic shell and round head, with a dark plastic screen over its cameras and other sensors, made ASIMO look a bit like an astronaut wearing a space suit and helmet (or, some said, an Imperial trooper from *Star Wars*). New ASIMO, an upgraded model, was introduced in 2005. Of all the artificial beings now in existence, this ASIMO probably comes closest to most people's idea of a robot.

New ASIMO does not just walk; it runs, at speeds of up to 3.7 miles (6 kilometers) per hour. It stands just over 51 inches (130 centimeters) tall, about the size of an average seven-year-old, and weighs 119 pounds (54 kilograms). This robot can push a cart, walk hand-in-hand with people, and recognize and receive instructions from people who hold a special electronic card. It can be programmed to serve as a receptionist or guide; in April 2006, in fact, it went to work as a receptionist at a Honda office in Japan.

Now that ASIMO is physically capable of performing many functions, Honda's next goal is to provide the robot with equally advanced intelligence, including the ability to make some decisions. The goal is for future versions of ASIMO to serve as caretakers, general household helpers, and office assistants. Honda wants to build "a humanoid robot that can help people and live together with people," the company has said.

ASIMOs have already functioned as entertainers and public-relations ambassadors. An ASIMO performs at Disneyland in California, for example, and when the queen of Denmark visited Japan in 2004, an ASIMO gave her flowers and joked with her in Danish. Such activities, together with appearances on talk shows and in commercials, have made ASIMO one of the world's most recognizable robots. It is still, however, a telerobot, controlled by a human operator. Independent action will have to wait until ASIMO's brain is as well developed as its body.

Artificial intelligence will be a necessary part of any robot that is capable of acting human. But why does a robot have to act human? One

ROBOSAPIEN MAKES ITS AUSTRALIAN DEBUT AT A DEPARTMENT STORE IN 2004. THIS AGILE TOY IS OPERATED WITH A CONTROL UNIT THAT USES INFRARED SIGNALS. ROBOSAPIEN CAN BE PROGRAMMED TO PERFORM A WIDE RANGE OF ACTIONS BUT IS NOT AUTONOMOUS.

school of robotics has turned away from the quest for AI and even from the use of high-powered computing in robots. It is called the BEAM school, which stands for "Biology, Electronics, Aesthetics, and Mechanics." The BEAM approach is to use the simplest possible parts to make basic, single-purpose robots. BEAM robots may contain low-power processors running simple programs, but for the most part, they are activated by simple sensors and switches, like William Grey Walter's tortoises in the 1940s. They are designed to perceive a stimulus—a piece of information about the world—and respond to it. Solarfly, for example, is a BEAM robot that has infrared sensors for eyes. Guided by input from these sensors, it moves toward the brightest object in its environment. Solarfly is powered by solar panels on its back that feed energy to its motor through two antennalike wires. Self-powering through solar energy is a goal for many BEAM robot designers, as is using recycled parts.

Some BEAM robots imitate the structure and behavior of animals. They creep along walls like mice, for example, or hop away from loud sounds. Robosapien, however, is a 14-inch (34-centimeter) humanoid toy robot built according to BEAM principles by a company headed by Mark Tilden, who is usually credited with founding the BEAM school of robotics. The battery-powered Robosapien responds to sound and touch signals with a variety of behaviors, including disco dancing, kung fu fighting, throwing things, and making caveman sounds. This energetic robot, much admired for its smooth and well-controlled movements, can perform for up to eight hours on one battery charge.

BEAM robots are mostly used to test new robotic motion systems, such as jumping, and as toys and educational tools. The most successful BEAM robots in the commercial marketplace are small cleaners for flat surfaces, such as floors and the bottoms of swimming pools. The world's best-selling household robot, for example, is Roomba, a disk-shaped BEAM robot that vacuums floors. The first generation of Roomba was put on the market in 2002 by iRobot, a company cofounded by Rodney Brooks, the creator of Cog. Since that time, successive models have added features and accessories, but Roomba—and its cousin Scooba, a floor-scrubbing robot introduced in 2005—still represent simple, functional robot design.

Roomba is basically a small, battery-operated vacuum cleaner with no handle or bag. Dirt is blown into a dustbin behind the vacuum motor, and after the robot has finished its work, the owner removes and

SPILLED CEREAL IS ALL IN A DAY'S WORK FOR A FLOOR-CLEANING ROBOT. MANY SIMPLE DEVICES, SUCH AS CLEANING AND SECURITY ROBOTS, PERFORM THEIR JOBS WITHOUT ACTIVE HUMAN SUPERVISION.

empties the dustbin. Sensors allow Roomba to navigate. It has sensors on its underside to tell it when it has started to go over a ledge, such as a stair. When one of these sensors is activated, Roomba backs away. Other sensors respond to infrared transmitting units called virtual walls. The owner places these units to mark the limits of the space where the robot is to clean; to the robot, they act as invisible barriers. Contact sensors tell the robot when it has bumped into a piece of furniture or a wall, which causes it to move off in a different direction. Roomba also has some basic communication tools. A cheery jingle is the sign that it has finished cleaning a room. When Roomba gets stuck in a corner or under a piece of furniture, it emits a plaintive sound.

Unlike some other robot vacuums with onboard computers, Roomba does not create an internal map of a room. Nor does it clean by starting at one point and moving back and forth in close lines, as a human would probably do. Instead, the Roomba's control circuits direct it to operate according to a set of specially written rules called heuristics, which are the principles that enable a system to learn or regulate itself. In the case of Roomba, its heuristics govern how the feedback from its actions determines its future actions. Guided by its heuristics, Roomba moves outward from its starting point in a spiral pattern, follows walls, and changes direction randomly when it bumps into something. The heuristics were designed to maximize the likelihood that Roomba would pass over each spot on the floor at least once. They do, however, contain an element of randomness. This means that the way Roomba cleans a floor cannot be predicted and will almost certainly change from one cleaning to the next. It also means that Roomba will probably clean some spots more than once and may miss a few spots altogether.

Unless stopped in mid-operation by its owner, the robot cleans each floor for a period of time that is determined roughly by the room's size. Because it is small and travels slowly, and because it duplicates its efforts in some places, Roomba takes longer to clean a floor than a human wielding a conventional vacuum cleaner would do. On the other hand, does it matter that Roomba is slower at vacuuming the floor than you would be? The robot is doing your work, after all. And cleaning floors is exactly the kind of repetitive, unglamorous work that visionaries once hoped robots would take off our human hands.

The maneuvers that Roomba uses to clean a floor could easily be applied to other tasks that require an area to be surveyed. Roomba's heuristics, in fact, were based on work that iRobot did to build a mine-sweeping robot for the U.S. Army. The shift from sweeping up dirt to detecting explosives is not surprising—in the world of robotics, technology that is developed for one purpose is often adapted to a multitude of others. Roombas themselves have spawned a small robotics subculture called Roombatics, in which people hack, or modify, Roombas, building on them to create their own robots.

Right now, research scientists, computer programmers, mechanical engineers, graduate students in robotics, high-school shop classes, and hobbyists of all ages are busy designing and building robots. These roboticists and enthusiasts share ideas and information on the Internet and at robot conventions and competitions. In the dynamic world of robotics, machines created as tools may morph into toys, and those invented for entertainment may lead the way to new developments in industrial, military, and household robots.

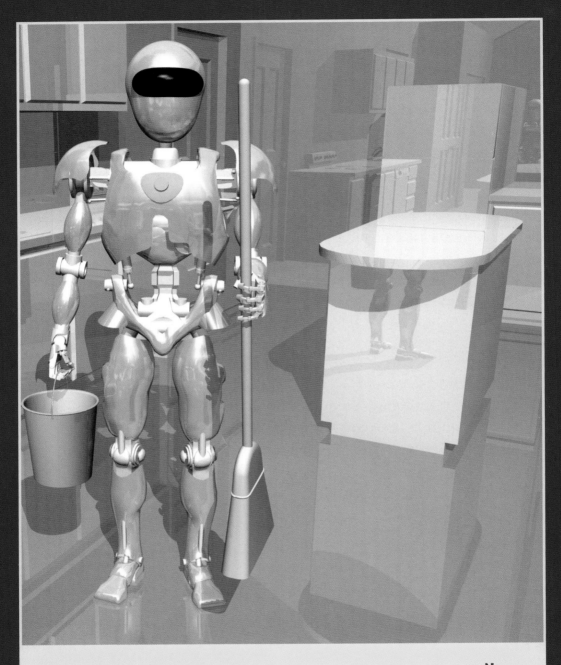

A COMPUTER MODEL OF A DOMESTIC ROBOT PREPARES TO GET BUSY ON A DIRTY FLOOR. NO SUCH ROBOT YET EXISTS, BUT SERVICE ROBOTS ARE BECOMING MORE VERSATILE ALL THE TIME.

# Robots for Work

**When the floor-scrubbing Scooba** came onto the market in 2005, a reviewer for the Web site technovelgy.com cheered—and pointed out that science-fiction author Robert A. Heinlein had imagined just such a robot worker in his 1956 book *The Door into Summer*. The Hired Girl, as Heinlein's fictional robot was called, cleaned floors "all day long and without supervision," looking for dirt "in search curves that could miss nothing." Afterward, Heinlein wrote, Hired Girl would "go to its stall and soak up a quick charge," just as some models of Roomba and Scooba are designed to dock themselves in their battery chargers when their cleaning is done. At last, science is beginning to catch up to science fiction. Can those flying cars be far behind?

Since 1961, when the first industrial robot, Unimate, was installed in a factory, working robots have become common, at least in some industries. Although it is impossible to say exactly how many robots there are in the world and what they are doing, in 2004 the United Nations Economic Commission for Europe (UNECE), together with the International Federation of Robotics (IFR), released the results of a robot census. According to their report, "World Robotics 2004," there were at least 600,000 multipurpose industrial robots in use throughout the world, and possibly as many as a million. Nearly half of them were in Japan. One interesting aspect of this figure was that in the previous survey, published in 2001, Japan had well over half of all industrial robots. The 2004

UNECE/IFR report revealed that Europe and North America were rapidly catching up with Japan in their use of robots in industry. Sales of industrial robots were also rising in developing economies such as China, Mexico, and Brazil, because the costs of human labor were going up while robot prices were remaining stable or falling.

The robot census also looked at household robots. About 610,000 units were in use worldwide in 2003, nearly all of them self-operating vacuum cleaners and lawn mowers. That number was projected to increase to about 4 million by 2007; in fact, that projection may have been surpassed. According to the UNECE and IFR, service robots were on the way to becoming everyday tools. The report said, "[Robots] will not only clean our floors, mow our lawns and guard our homes but they will also assist old and handicapped people with sophisticated interactive equipment, carry out surgery, inspect pipes and sites that are hazardous to people, fight fire and bombs and be used in many other applications. . . . Huge military investment in service robots will give spin-off effects both for the market of professional service robots and for the market of consumer products."

Have you ridden in a car lately? If so, you have experienced the handiwork of industrial robots. Virtually every automotive plant in the world, apart from very small specialty manufacturers, uses robots on its assembly line. Industrial robots typically have the following features: at least one axis of motion (a movable joint, such as a shoulder, elbow, or wrist); end effectors (tools that can be attached to the "hand" end of the mechanism); and the ability to be reprogrammed for different tasks. Most also have some ability to sense their environment.

Many industrial robots now have "eyes" in the form of cameras or laser rangefinders for precision targeting and inspection. Vision-guided end-effector placement—in other words, letting the robot see where to point the screwdriver—has the advantage of remaining highly accurate over time. As wear gradually causes the mechanical parts of a robot's arm to shift slightly, its vision sensors can correct for this drift.

The task most often assigned to robots is welding car bodies and

ROBOTIC ARMS WELD A CAR FRAME AT A SATURN PLANT IN TENNESSEE. WELDING IS ONE OF THE JOBS COMMONLY TURNED OVER TO INDUSTRIAL ROBOTS.

other pieces of equipment together. Unable to be burned by flying sparks and capable of positioning an arc welder at the exact same spot thousands of times, robots are ideal for such jobs. Robots also assemble electronic equipment, such as computers and cell phones—and, of course, robots. Robotic vision is essential for precise targeting when robots work with tiny components in small spaces, and robots with visual capabilities also perform quality-control inspections of finished products. Units that are equipped with laser scanners can detect even tiny irregularities.

Remote-controlled robots, or telerobots, are already being used to do some of humankind's most unpleasant, dangerous, and difficult jobs. The German-made MAKKRO, for example, is a 6.5-foot (2-meter) wheeled robot that is shaped and segmented like a large earthworm. Fitted with lights and cameras, MAKKRO crawls through sewer lines, inspecting them for leaks and blockages, while its operators observe from afar in relative comfort.

Robots are also very useful for handling radioactive or toxic material, and for disposing of mines and bombs. At a nuclear power plant in Chernobyl, Ukraine, for example, robots have been used for inspections and repairs inside the reactor where an explosion occurred in 1986. The interior of the reactor remains highly radioactive, a perilous environment for humans, even if they wear protective suits. Robots, however, can navigate it safely. One of the first robotic tools used at Chernobyl was a remote-controlled toy tank. Researchers attached lights and a camera to it and sent it to get pictures of the bottom of the reactor core. Other remote-controlled devices have cleared rubble from the site, monitored radiation levels, and even sprayed glue on surfaces to control the spread of radioactive dust. In 1999 a U.S.-built robot named *Pioneer* was donated to Ukraine to help in the task of studying and repairing the shield that was constructed around the damaged reactor after the explosion. Built to navigate hazards such as pools of radioactive water and streams of melted reactor fuel, *Pioneer* was one of many robots from Japan, the United States, and Europe that have worked at

Chernobyl, the world's most hazardous nuclear site. Advances in AI will allow robots to perform such tasks with greater and greater independence.

Although you may be perfectly willing to let a robot install radiation meters inside a damaged nuclear reactor, would you let one remove your tonsils? Robots are not yet performing surgery on their own, but doctors have begun using remotely operated telerobots in surgery. The da Vinci robotic surgical system, developed by Yale University, consists of a pedestal to which five robot arms are attached, each capable of holding small versions of surgical tools. A human surgeon operates da Vinci by sitting at a console and manipulating his hands on a set of controls; the robotic arms copy his movements. In fact, the robot can be programmed to filter out the human operator's muscle tremors.

Da Vinci's microtools are too small to be directly used by a human surgeon. Using the robot arms, though, the surgeon can operate through very tiny holes or incisions in the patient's body, resulting in reduced trauma and healing time for patients. For internal surgery, the surgeon can send a tiny camera inside the patient on one of the robot arms and then use its video feed to guide the other tools through the operation. The system can be operated from across the room or, by means of a computer connection, from across the globe. A surgeon in New York, for example, has used da Vinci to remove the gallbladder of a patient in France. Today da Vinci is just another tool in the arsenal of a skilled and highly trained human, but in the future it, or a robot like it, may be programmed with the ability to carry out some surgeries on its own.

Service robots will soon outnumber industrial robots, if they have not done so already, led by the scooting hordes of Roombas and other robotic floor cleaners. Personal service robots, which some marketers call helperbots, are beginning to take a variety of forms. Robots already exist that can carry trays, keep schedules and issue reminders of appointments, and respond to simple voice commands, such as "Come here," "Call doctor," or "Call police." They can also monitor home security, just as electronic alarm systems do, with sensors to

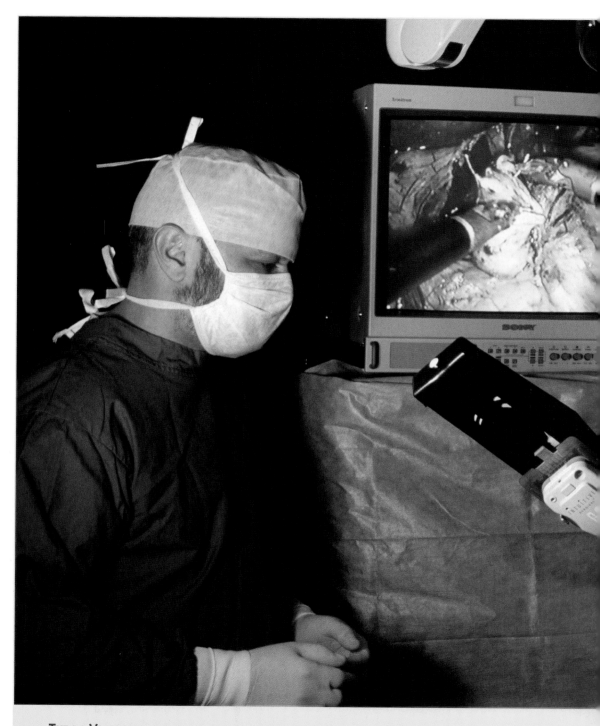

THE DA VINCI SURGICAL ROBOT LETS A SURGEON MANIPULATE TINY TOOLS THROUGH
SMALL INCISIONS IN THE PATIENT'S BODY. ONE TOOL, A FLEXIBLE VIEWER CALLED AN

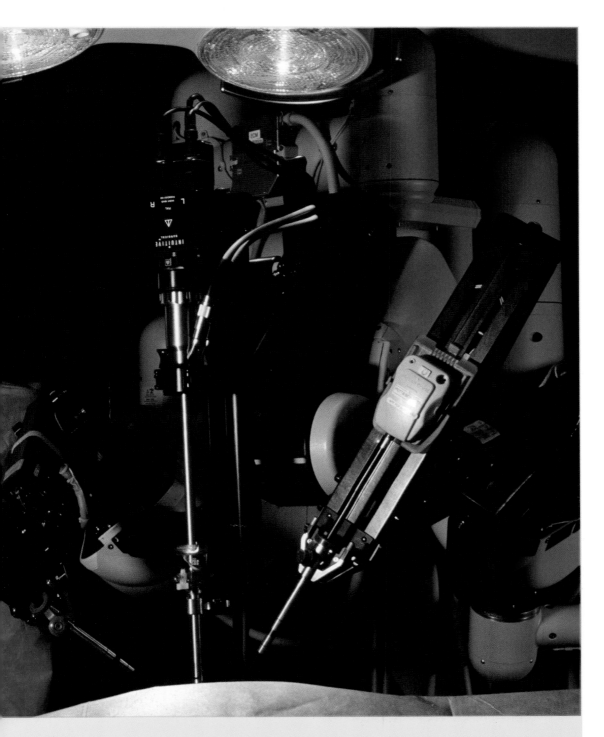

ENDOSCOPE, TRANSMITS A CLOSE-UP IMAGE OF THE SURGERY TO THE TELEVISION MONITOR IN THE BACKGROUND.

detect fires, gas leaks, or intrusions and programmed instructions on the appropriate responses.

The service robot is becoming increasingly useful as a home companion for elderly or disabled people; this is expected to be one of the fastest-developing and fastest-selling categories of robots in the coming decades. Gecko Systems already markets a CareBot to assist in the care of children and the elderly. Mitsubishi's Wakamaru robot can recognize faces and use the Internet. Pearl, under development at Carnegie Mellon University, is being designed specifically for eldercare, with a sympathetic face and a body that can serve as a walker, guide, or grocery cart. As the capabilities of such robots increase, the robots will be able to start doing household chores such as food preparation and cleaning. At some point in the future—although probably not for many years—people may be able to purchase robot "butlers." These advanced general-purpose robots will most likely be humanoid in form, to make them appealing to potential buyers. The robots will competently handle many aspects of household life, from home security to shopping for the family's vacation airline tickets on the Web.

Consumers may want their home robots to have friendly faces and familiar forms, but those considerations do not apply to another growing family of working machines, security robots. Security robots are not new. They have been around since the mid-twentieth century, when they came into use as moving security alarms and remote-controlled cameras at power plants and factories. Since that time, control circuits and microprocessors have steadily grown smaller and more powerful, and programming has become more sophisticated. As a result, today's security 'bots are packed with features.

Two widely used security robots are MOSRO and OFRO, autonomous units made by the German company Robowatch Technologies. MOSRO is a 4-foot (1.2-meter) steel cylinder on a wheeled base. A red dome on top not only serves as a warning flasher when illuminated but also houses a videocamera and a fingerprint scanner. MOSRO can be fitted with more than two hundred sensors for detecting motion,

HELPING TO CARE FOR CHILDREN, ELDERLY PEOPLE, AND THE DISABLED IS ONE ROLE THAT ROBOTS ARE LIKELY TO FILL IN THE FUTURE; THE FIRST SUCH ROBOTS ARE ALREADY ON THE MARKET. IF ROBOTS' ROLE AS CARETAKERS IS TO EXPAND, PEOPLE WILL NEED A HIGH DEGREE OF TRUST IN THEIR MECHANICAL COMPANIONS.

smoke, or gas, depending upon the customer's needs. It can also be equipped to utter warnings in twenty languages. MOSRO was designed for indoor use in sites such as malls and factories, to make it easier for the human security staff to maintain full coverage of the site. In recent years, increased public security needs have caused many MOSROs to be deployed at airports.

OFRO, mounted on caterpillar treads and housed in a weatherproof casing, is MOSRO's outdoor counterpart, suitable for patrolling airfields and military bases. OFRO looks like a small white tank with a long, ostrichlike neck. A camera, heat sensor, and radio equipment are mounted in the robot's head, which can rotate in a complete circle.

Robot evolution is demonstrated in Robart, a security robot developed by the U.S. Navy. Robart I, introduced in 1980, had sensors to avoid collisions but could not map its environment—it could only navigate along a preprogrammed route. It could detect indications of possible intrusion but could not filter out false alarms from genuine threats. In 1982 the navy adopted Robart II, which continued to be developed for the next decade. This robot could map its immediate environment, locate itself on a world map, and combine input from various sensors to calculate the probability that a given disturbance was a false alarm. The navy is now working on Robart III, which will be able to target intruders with a built-in airgun that fires nonlethal darts.

The world's military forces have been using robots for years—although not as long as comic-book artist Paul Guinan wants people to think. Guinan is the creator of Boilerplate, an Internet hoax. With invented documents and digitally manipulated photographs, Guinan contrived the tale of a robot soldier, built in the Victorian era, that fought in the Spanish-American War and World War I. Hardy, brave, durable, and uncomplaining, Boilerplate seemed like the perfect soldier. Alas, it and other "Victorian robots" described on Guinan's Web site are purely fictional. If a robot capable of independent military action had existed as long ago as the 1890s, the field of robotics would now be much, much more advanced than it is—either that, or the

U.S. MILITARY FORCES USE PORTABLE, REMOTE-CONTROLLED ROBOTS IN THE WAR ON TERROR. THE **THROWBOT** PICTURED HERE IS THE SIZE OF A SODA CAN AND EQUIPPED WITH TINY CAMERAS. SMALL REMOTE-CONTROLLED ROBOTS EQUIPPED WITH SENSING DEVICES CAN SERVE MANY MILITARY AND ESPIONAGE PURPOSES, SUCH AS SEARCHING FOR BOMBS AND BOOBY TRAPS BEFORE TROOPS ENTER AN AREA OR INFILTRATING ENEMY TERRITORY.

robots would have killed us all!

Military robotics research focuses not on creating the robot soldiers that appear in many movies but on telerobots, which have already proven their usefulness and versatility in combat. Unmanned aerial vehicles, for example, are small, light, maneuverable aircraft flown by operators on the ground—in short, they are very sophisticated model airplanes, although the military usually calls them UAVs or drones. The Predator UAV can spend up to twenty-four hours in the air at a time, recording the terrain with an array of videocameras. Some of them can capture details as small as a car or a person from distances as great as 56 miles (90 kilometers). It and similar flying telerobots are perfect for advance scouting of new or hostile territory. UAVs can also be used to identify targets and then "paint" the targets with laser light to guide incoming bombs to their intended destinations. The Predator can not only identify targets but also launch missiles to destroy them.

Telerobots work with ground troops in combat situations. In its early–twenty-first-century wars in Afghanistan and Iraq, the U.S. military has used an array of robotic aids, from the car-sized Gladiator, armored and equipped to carry cameras and weapons through battlefields, to the backpack-sized PackBot, used for clearing bombs and booby traps out of caves and buildings. In 2004 the U.S. military was using about 150 robots in Iraq and Afghanistan; by early 2007 that number had risen to more than five thousand. Some were designed with special senses, such as Fido, a telerobot developed by iRobot that has built-in sensors for detecting explosives, such as car bombs. Others may be used in combat. In 2004 the U.S. Army announced that it had begun fitting some Talons—small robots with caterpillar tracks and manipulator arms that are used to defuse bombs—with machine guns. The guns could be aimed by computer-aided targeting programs and fired via remote control by an operator who would monitor the feed from the robot's videocamera (complete with zoom lenses and night-vision capabilities). Known as Special Weapons Observation Reconnaissance Detection Systems (SWORDS), these armed robots were intended to be used in firefights against Iraqi insurgents, giving U.S. forces the ability to direct accurate fire at the enemy while lessening the danger to American soldiers.

Big Dog is a robot being developed for possible military use. Intended to carry soldiers' packs and other supplies over rough terrain, Big Dog stands 27 inches (69 centimeters) high and has four legs equipped with joints and springs. Its creator, roboticist Marc Raibert, designed it to avoid obstacles, climb rocky slopes, and jump ditches as wide as 3 feet (1 meter). Other robotic vehicles are being developed for the U.S. Defense Department as part of the Future Combat Systems program. Some of them, like Big Dog, are intended to be autonomous, or semiautonomous, not teleoperated. It may be years before these advanced military machines roll out. In the meantime, however, robot vehicles are also being used in an activity that, like war, is hazardous and full of surprises. That activity is exploration.

Robots have boldly gone where no one has gone before. They have proved to be invaluable for bringing back information from places that are difficult, dangerous, or impossible for humans to visit. Often called probes, these remote-controlled, semiautonomous, or autonomous devices have traveled to the depths of the sea, the craters of fiery volcanoes, and the farthest reaches of the solar system.

Since the 1960s scientists have used small submarines called submersibles to explore the ocean depths. When a marine biologist, salvage diver, or maker of underwater documentaries wants to enter a place that is too small for the submersible, such as an octopus's cave or the hold of a sunken ship, he or she can call on telerobots called remotely operated vehicles (ROVs). Controlled through cables by someone inside the submersible (or, sometimes, aboard a ship on the surface), an ROV can maneuver cameras and other equipment around corners, into crevices in the Arctic ice pack, or down the walls of undersea cliffs.

In addition to their role in scientific exploration and research, ROVs with robot arms, hands, and tools also assist in undersea rescue and repair operations, mine-clearing, and commercial operations such as laying undersea fiber-optic cables and performing maintenance on mid-ocean oil rigs. Filmmaker James Cameron, the director of *Titanic* (1997), used two specially built, small ROVs—nicknamed Jake and

A ROBOT ARM RETRIEVES PIECES OF A WINDOW FROM THE SUNKEN PASSENGER LINER TITANIC, NEARLY 2.5 MILES (4 KILOMETERS) BELOW THE OCEAN'S SURFACE.

Elwood after the heroes of *The Blues Brothers*—to film the inside of the sunken *Titanic* for a documentary about the ship.

Autonomous underwater vehicles, or AUVs, have been called "ROVs with brains." These devices are programmed to operate on their own, at least to some extent. One of the most successful AUVs is Autosub, built by the Southampton Oceanography Centre in Great Britain. Although Autosub lacks arms and cannot perform any actions, it is capable of navigating on its own, without remote control, for extended periods, and then returning to its starting point. Autosub has been used for surveying missions everywhere from Antarctica to Loch Ness (where it searched for minerals, not monsters—but found no evidence of a monster).

The crater of a volcano is usually less dangerous to human life than the bottom of the sea. After all, there is air in a volcano. But when that air fills with poisonous volcanic gases, flying bits of molten lava, or falling ash, the crater becomes distinctly inhospitable. For that reason, volcanologists and robot scientists have collaborated on several projects to develop robots that can perform some of the dangerous tasks of volcano research, such as measuring temperatures and collecting soil and gas samples from within craters, or performing maintenance on the monitoring instruments that are permanently positioned there.

With high temperatures, uneven terrain, and frequent ground tremors, volcanoes have proven to be difficult for robots to master. During the 1990s, a pair of pioneering, eight-legged, spider-style volcano 'bots came to untimely ends. Just a few minutes into its first mission, Dante I lost its footing and fell into lava in Mount Erebus, a volcano in Antarctica.

*Dante II*, equipped with more versatile climbing skills, did quite a bit better when it descended into the crater of Alaska's Mount Spurr. A cable called a tether linked *Dante II* to a portable power generator that supplied it with energy, while a satellite relay system carried commands from the operators, who were 60 miles (100 kilometers) away, out of the danger zone. It took *Dante II* a couple of days to reach the floor of the volcano. Despite being struck by several rolling or falling rocks, the robot

*DANTE II* DESCENDED INTO AN ALASKAN VOLCANO BUT COULD NOT GET OUT ON ITS OWN. ALTHOUGH VOLCANOES HAVE PROVED TO BE TREACHEROUS TERRAIN FOR ROBOTS, THE QUEST CONTINUES FOR A MACHINE THAT CAN AID IN EXPLORING THESE DANGEROUS SITES.

crept around in smoke, snow, and steam, guided by operators who had great difficulty interpreting the images from its cameras. For three days, *Dante II* collected samples, took measurements, and made its way around fuming vents. Once *Dante II* had begun to climb back up the slope to leave the crater, however, things started to go wrong. The power cable short-circuited, ash confused Dante's navigational laser scanner, and, during an attempted airlift, the cable broke, sending the robot plummeting back down into the crater. Although *Dante II* was recovered from Mount Spurr, it did not return to active volcano duty.

Projects are under way to develop other robots for use in and around volcanoes. In Japan, an autonomous unmanned helicopter developed by the Yamaha Corporation is used to monitor conditions at Mount Usu on the island of Hokkaido. In the early 2000s, a multinational European team developed Robovolc, a wheeled telerobot that may be used for volcano studies. A number of other researchers have used volcanoes to test robot mechanisms and designs for use in the extreme conditions of Mars or at other sites within the solar system. And NASA, one of the developers of the Dante robots, has also designed and operated two of the world's most famous robot explorers, *Spirit* and *Opportunity*, the Martian rovers.

The twin robots were launched toward the red planet in 2003 in two unmanned spacecraft. At the time, *Spirit* and *Opportunity* were among the most complex robots that had ever been made, equipped with multiple cameras, sensors, tools, recording and communicating equipment, onboard computers, motors and mechanisms to operate their wheels, extendable arms, and solar recharging panels.

The spacecraft reached Mars in January 2004. After *Spirit* was dropped to a landing in a crater, millions of people around the world logged onto NASA's Web site to follow the Mars scientists' efforts to free the remote-controlled rover from an airbag that had failed to deflate, and then to move it safely down the ramp of its landing gear. Finally, after a suspenseful week, *Spirit* rolled onto Martian soil. The first thing it did was start examining a nearby rock. Almost at once, problems with the software threatened to derail *Spirit*'s mission before it had really gotten started. Operators were able to transmit new software to the rover, however, and *Spirit* carried on. *Opportunity*, on the opposite side of the planet, performed well from the start.

NASA hoped that the two Mars rovers would operate for three months after landing on the planet, and cover at least 500 or 600 yards (457 or 549 meters) each. As of early 2007, both rovers remained in

ONE OF THE MARS ROVERS ROLLS INTO ACTION, PREPARING TO GET A SAMPLE OF A MARTIAN ROCK.

operation, still exploring and transmitting new information despite a few mechanical problems. They had outlasted their "warranty" by years and covered far more ground than anyone had dreamed possible; *Opportunity* had covered more than seventeen times the hoped-for distance. Together the rovers had revealed a wealth of information about the soil, air, weather, and geology of Mars. In late 2006, long after the point at which NASA expected its mission to have ended, *Spirit* discovered signs of past water in a patch of Martian soil, another piece of evidence that water once flowed on Mars.

Robot explorers are not cheap, but it costs far less to send a robot, or a whole pack of them, to another planet than it does to send a human crew there. People may one day resume manned space exploration— but wherever we go, we are certain to send robots ahead first, and to take other robots with us.

ROBOTS MARCHED INTO THE WORLD OF TOYS LONG BEFORE THEY MADE THEIR MARK ON INDUSTRY OR
EXPLORATION. TOY ROBOTS HAVE BEEN POPULAR SINCE THE 1930S.

# Robots for Fun

**The first robot toy was sold** in 1932, a dozen years after the word *robot* was coined. It was the Buddy "L" Robotoy, a green and red dump truck with a robot driver. A few years later, the first freestanding toy robot, Lilliput, became available. Boxy and yellow, with painted-on dials and legs that moved the robot forward in a stiff gait when its clockwork mechanism was wound up with a key, Lilliput was the ancestor of a vast and varied population of toy robots.

Today, toy robots are more numerous than ever. Some of them are mere dolls or simple clockwork mechanisms. This category includes the action figures of well-known fictional robots such as R2D2, C3PO, the evil Dalek cyborgs from the British television series *Dr. Who*, and Bender, the crass but charismatic robot dreamed up by Matt Groening, the creator of *The Simpsons*, for his animated comedy *Futurama*. Others, however, are real robots—complete with computers, sensors, and other advanced features—that can be bought ready-made or built from kits or parts. Students and hobbyists build their own 'bots for robot sports and design competitions. Buyers make custom modifications to purchased robots. Each year, new models of companion and pet robots, enhanced with more and better features, reach the market. Just as robots have steadily moved into the world of work, they have also found a place in the world of entertainment.

After World War II ended in 1945, toy robots saw a surge in popularity, with dozens of new models entering the market. One of the strangest robots from this era was made in Japan. The robot itself is not particularly unusual. It was manufactured from tinplate, an inexpensive material used for many early toy robots, and had clockwork legs and stenciled dials. Its distinctive features were its name, Atomic Man, and its packaging, a box that showed the robot striding through a destroyed city. In the background is the deadly mushroom cloud of an atomic bomb, like those that the United States dropped on the Japanese cities of Hiroshima and Nagasaki in 1945. Marketed as a toy, Atomic Man carried powerful images of a recent horror. A similar image of a robot in a devastated city, but without the mushroom cloud, appeared on the box of Zoomer, a battery-operated robot manufactured in Japan in the 1950s.

One of the earliest battery-operated toy robots was Robert, first produced by the Ideal Toy Corporation in 1954. Instead of legs, 14-inch-tall (35.5-centimeter-tall) Robert had a solid lower half. Using a remote-control device that was attached to the robot by a cable, the operator could make Robert move forward, backward, and sideways. As the robot moved, its arms swung back and forth and its eyes lit up. A hand crank in the robot's back activated its voicebox, making it say, "I am Robert the Robot, mechanical man. Drive me, steer me, wherever you can." By the standards of the video game generation, Robert may not seem very impressive, but in the 1950s it was a sensation. To this day it remains one of the best-selling toy robots ever created.

The similarly named Robby the Robot from *Forbidden Planet,* another popular robot character, inspired numerous toys over the years. Robby models were even provided with accessories; in the 1950s, for example, Robby was equipped with a road-building roller. Apparently, the toy's designers thought there was a chance that a highly advanced, intelligent robot from the future might take up highway construction.

In 1982, the Japanese company Popy/Bandai introduced its Machine-Robo and Godaikin toy robots. The MachineRobo series was a set of robots that, with a few simple adjustments of their components, transformed into other objects, such as a sports car, tank, or helicopter.

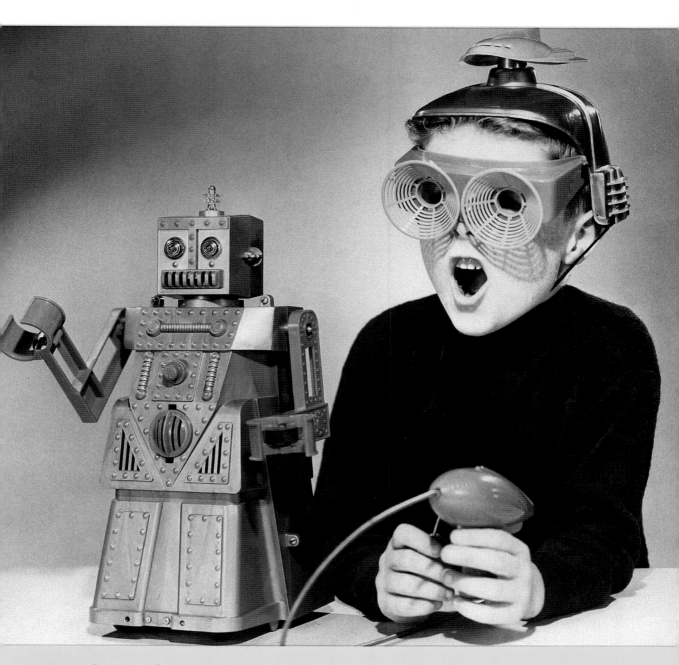

ROBERT THE ROBOT, A HIGHLY SUCCESSFUL WALKING, TALKING TOY, IS DEMONSTRATED BY A BOY WEARING A 1959 TOY DESIGNER'S IDEA OF A SPACE HELMET AND GOGGLES.

The Godaikin models were robots that separated into three smaller robots and could then be reassembled into a single figure. The concept of robots changing into other things hit its stride two years later with Transformers, called "robots in disguise," and GoBots. Both sets of toys inspired television programs, and the Transformers eventually appeared in a movie.

The Transformers were also one of the inspirations behind "the world's biggest entertainment robot," Robosaurus. Created in 1989, Robosaurus is a giant mechanical dinosaur that transforms into a large trailer to be pulled around the country for appearances at fairs, monster truck rallies, and other events. More than 40 feet (12 meters) tall and weighing about 26 tons, capable of breathing fire and crushing cars with its bare claws, Robosaurus is an impressive feat of engineering, but it is not a true robot. It is driven at all times by a rider who sits inside its head.

In recent years, robot toys have acquired a host of new abilities. One of them is spoken communication, a robotic skill that is still in the early stages of development. People in a research division of Apple Computers, it is said, used to wear T-shirts that proclaimed, "I Helped Apple Wreck A Nice Beach." Read the slogan aloud a couple of times, and you may realize that you are saying, "I helped Apple recognize speech." Speech-recognition technology is designed to give computers (and, by extension, robots) the ability to hear, understand, and respond to spoken commands. The T-shirt illustrates the difficulty of the task—the same sequence of sounds can have more than one meaning. Not only that, but people speak with distinctive rhythms, accents, and habits of pronunciation. Getting a robot to reliably understand even a limited menu of spoken words is not easy. Still, speech recognition has developed to the point where it can be used in everyday applications, such as automated telephone-answering systems. It is also incorporated in a number of robots, including some robot pets.

Robot pets are designed to offer some of the features of dogs and cats (and even fish), without the messy necessity of having to clean, feed,

Tired of cleaning up after that messy dog of yours? Try a robot pup. Such inventions may make us wonder whether a mechanical creation will ever truly take the place of a living animal—or person.

and care for live animals. One robot pet was the AIBO dog, introduced by Sony in 1999 and discontinued in 2006. The later models could not only recognize nearly a hundred voice commands but could also recognize faces and play soccer.

From the start of the toy robot craze in the mid-twentieth century, there were kids who took apart their toy robots, studied the innards, and said, "I could make that." This do-it-yourself spirit got a big boost in the early 1980s, when the kit robots entered the market. Like model aircraft, kit robots blur the distinctions among toys, hobbies, experiments, and educational tools. Today, anyone who wants a robot can build one—not just a toy with movable arms and wind-up legs, but a true robot that navigates independently, has electronic sensors and control circuits, and may even include a microprocessor and programmable software.

Kit robots are available for every skill and interest level, and in every price range. Some simple kits use snap-together plastic parts and basic electronic circuits to produce small, buglike 'bots. The LEGO company, maker of snap-together building bricks, has combined its building-block materials with motors, sensors, and software in the Mindstorms robot kits. Cybot kits, created by cybernetics researchers at Britain's Reading University, produce tortoiselike wheeled robots that can be programmed through a connection with a PC. With Hexapod kits, users can build six-legged walking robots. There are even kits for making humanoid robots that can walk, recognize voices and faces, and access the Internet wirelessly.

The do-it-yourself urge can take strange turns. After Californian Marc Thorpe tried and failed to build a radio-controlled vacuum cleaner, he was left with some mobile robot bases. He decided to attach power tools and chainsaws to them and let them attack each other. The idea caught on among Thorpe's friends, and in 1994 he held a robot battle in an arena in San Francisco. After several such events, the idea was adapted—without Thorpe's permission, which led to a lawsuit—into a British television series called *Robot Wars,* which ran from 1998 to

ROBOTS HAVE BEEN PROGRAMMED TO PLAY SOCCER.

QRIO, A ROBOT PROTOTYPE DEVELOPED BY SONY BUT NEVER MARKETED, COULD NOT ONLY RUN BUT DANCE. SEVERAL OF THE PROTOTYPES HAVE SHOWN OFF THEIR MOVES IN MUSIC VIDEOS.

SQUIRT IS A MINI-ROBOT DESIGNED BY THE MASSACHUSETTS INSTITUTE OF TECHNOLOGY AS PART OF A TEAM OF SMALL "INSECTOID" ROBOTS FOR MILITARY RECONNAISSANCE. SQUIRT'S JOB IS TO SEEK OUT A DARK PLACE AND HIDE, COMING OUT ONLY TO INVESTIGATE LOUD NOISES.

# The Next Big (or Little) Thing in Robotics

When Nikola Tesla demonstrated his remote-controlled robot boat in 1898, he hoped that the navy would be interested enough in its possibilities to license the technology or finance further development. That did not work out as Tesla had hoped, but modern inventors may be more fortunate. Today the military searches for worthy robots. Computer scientists and roboticists working on self-driving cars, for example, have a shot at a cash prize and a military research contract.

In 2004 the Defense Advanced Research Projects Agency (DARPA), which is part of the U.S. Defense Department, held a robot race it called the Grand Challenge. It invited participants to enter autonomous, or self-driving, vehicles in a 150-mile (240-kilometer) race over difficult terrain in the Mojave Desert of the American Southwest. DARPA's goal was to identify technology that held promise for future military vehicles that could navigate on their own without endangering human drivers.

To complete the Grand Challenge course, vehicles required sensor and guidance systems that would recognize obstacles such as rocks, gullies, and hairpin turns, and enable the vehicles to negotiate these obstacles. The sensing systems used videocameras, laser rangefinders, infrared sensors, radar, or some combination of those capabilities. Vehicles also had to be programmed to follow the course using global positioning systems (GPS) for navigation. Finally, they would have to

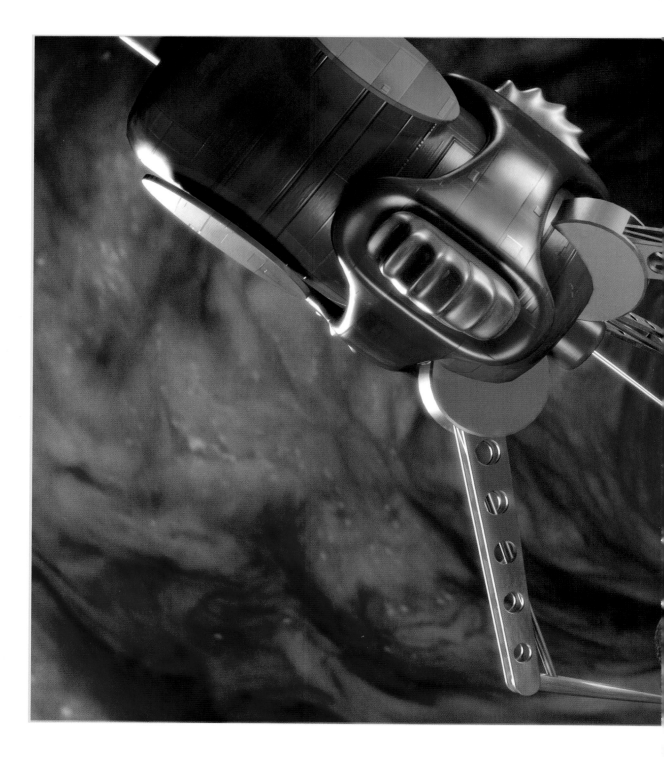

A MICROSCOPICALLY TINY MEDICAL NANOBOT INJECTS A DRUG INTO CANCER CELLS (SHOWN IN RED) IN A HUMAN BODY. SOMEDAY SUCH VISIONS MAY BECOME REALITY.

of today's vastly more limited technological capabilities, such robot powers would seem to illustrate a statement made in 1972 by British science-fiction writer Arthur C. Clarke: "Any sufficiently advanced technology is indistinguishable from magic."

Swarm robotics is another fast-developing area of research that seems likely to grow in the future. It is concerned with controlling systems that are made up of multiple agents, large or small. The goal of swarm robotics is not to make a robot that looks, acts, or thinks like a human being, or even a primate. Instead, social insects, such as ants and bees, are the model for this school of robotics. For some tasks, many relatively simple robots working together are a better solution than a single, more-sophisticated robot. James McLurkin's milk-carton-sized robots are an example.

McLurkin holds an advanced degree from MIT's computer science program. In early 2007 he participated in a DARPA experiment to test distributed robots, in which computing and communication power, as well as responsibility for completing a task, are distributed among many units working together—swarms, in other words. McLurkin sent a hundred of his robots into an empty building. Their mission was to locate and explore every room, and they performed better than expected. The robots were equipped with what McLurkin calls frontier-guided exploration software, which lets teams of robots guide each other through new territory, starting with the closest points and moving out from there, each robot building on what the others learn. Such robots could one day be sent into disaster sites, after an earthquake, for example, to search for survivors. They could also explore caves, buildings in combat zones, and other potentially dangerous locations, serving as advance scouts and information-gatherers for their human operators.

Millibots are swarm robots being developed by Carnegie Mellon University for DARPA. Each member of this family of miniature robots is between 2 and 2.25 inches (5 and 6 centimeters) long and is designed for a different function. SonarBot, for example, uses sonar to scan for obstacles at distances of up to 20 inches (50 centimeters). PyroBot uses a heat detector to locate fires, CameraBot makes color or black-and-white video recordings, and DirrsBot (short for "digital infrared ranging sensor") locates walls and doors. The Millibot research and development team hopes to create software that will allow these computerized minirobots to pool information and work together as a team. In the future, swarms of even smaller robots, closer in size to actual bees or ants, may have uses in such fields as exploration, security, espionage, and safety inspections inside dams and pipelines.

Insects and their larval forms are the inspiration for another possible trend in future robotics: soft robots. Such robots could squeeze through tight places, bend in any direction, and possibly survive falls or other accidents better than rigid ones. Today's stiff, jointed robots move like hard-shell crabs, but soft robots are modeled on more flexible creatures. Sprawlita, a hand-sized, six-legged robot that is part of the large family of Sprawl robots developed at Stanford University, has flexible feet made of nylon tubing and hip joints that can flatten. Sprawlita runs a bit like a cockroach, which was the model for the engineering of its locomotion.

Caterpillars are the cue for Barry Trimmer and other researchers at a Tufts University project called Biomimetic Technologies for Soft-Bodied Robots (*biomimetic* means "imitating life"). They are looking into the possibility of soft-bodied robots made like caterpillars, which are squishy and stretchy—or, as the scientists working on the project prefer to say, elastic. The researchers are studying how caterpillars' nervous systems work, hoping to learn how the fairly simple organic wiring controls the highly flexible body. They are also building preliminary models of robots based on the design of the caterpillar. The robots' bodies are hollow tubes of silicone rubber. Wire springs act as muscles, contracting in response to electrical currents and then returning to their normal shape, pulled by the skin, when the current stops. If Trimmer and the other researchers are successful in creating a robot that can move like a caterpillar, such devices might one day be used for tasks such as repairing hard-to-reach machinery or even entering the human body to gather information about medical conditions.

THE CENTIBOTS ARE A 100-UNIT TEAM BUILT IN THE EARLY 2000S TO STUDY THE USE OF DISTRIBUTED, OR SWARM, ROBOTICS IN URBAN SURVEILLANCE. ONE GROUP OF CENTIBOTS CAN SURVEY A BUILDING, POOLING THEIR INFORMATION TO CREATE A MAP. A SECOND GROUP SEARCHES THE BUILDING FOR A TARGET, COMMUNICATING WITH EACH OTHER AND WITH THEIR CONTROLLER.

Energetic autonomy is another area of robotics that is likely to see an increase in research in the coming years. An energetic autonomous robot is one that can produce all of the energy it needs to operate, so that it can remain self-sufficient indefinitely. Solar panels are one route to energy autonomy, although they often require adjustment by human operators. Biomass conversion is another route. EcoBots, developed by the Bristol Robotics Laboratory in Britain, run on energy from fuel cells powered by microbes. The microbes feed on biological matter fed to the EcoBots, which may one day be able to scavenge for their own fuel. In 2004, EcoBot II remained continuously active for twelve days after consuming eight house flies. Robots using similar technology could eventually serve two purposes, combining housecleaning, for example, with garbage disposal.

A robot that can power itself would be handy. So would a robot that can repair itself, or at least adjust to changes in its physical condition. Researchers at Cornell University may have achieved a breakthrough in that direction with Starfish, a four-footed robot developed for future use on missions to distant destinations, such as Mars or its moons. A robot that loses a limb or suffers other damage in an unreachable locale—as *Spirit* did when one of its wheels became inoperable on Mars—may jeopardize the mission's success.

Starfish is a prototype of a robot that observes itself, creates an internal model of its own movements and capabilities, and constantly tests the accuracy of the model. If its sensors tell it that something has changed, it alters the model to match its new sensory input, and this in turn alters its actions. When the researchers removed one of Starfish's legs, for example, the robot did not stop walking. It changed its gait, adapting to new circumstances. According to Josh Bongard, one of Starfish's designers, the robot's creators tried to give it a sense of curiosity and play. "[Starfish] always tries to perform some action, to move in a new way, to give it new information about its body," Bongard says. In young animals, including humans, play and constant movement are also vital to developing control over the body and its abilities. Starfish may be a (three-legged) step on the road to developing a robot that participates in its own growth.

Humans are not the only ones who are designing new robots. At Brandeis University, researchers have developed a computer program that designs robots and then instructs a machine to fabricate them. The program uses the principles of genetics and evolution to produce robots that are capable of locomotion. First, it combines basic elements of structure with networks of switches to produce many possible designs, then it evaluates the designs for survival fitness, and finally it selects the most fit designs to be fabricated out of plastic. The products, called genetically organized lifelike electromechanics, or GOLEMs, are small and can do only one thing: move. Most GOLEMs look nothing like the robots that have been designed by a human, but a few of them have structures reminiscent of natural organisms, such as crabs or snakes.

The GOLEM project is a step toward the day when robots do not simply build other robots that have been designed by humans, but start designing their own robot creations. The robots they make will almost certainly be different from those we build ourselves. Robot-designed robots may not only shed light on how robots solve problems but also enlarge our notions of what a robot can be and do.

Experts at the Department of Energy's Idaho National Laboratory (INL), where a number of research projects involving humanoid robots are under way, have contemplated the possibility that, as one report states, "humans and humanoids may evolve along separate trajectories such that it may never make sense to equate human and humanoid intelligence. Most likely, humans and humanoids will continue to be good at different things." In this view, robots are not imitation humans—they are more like an evolving species with their own brand of intelligence, which perhaps will never be like our own.

# Humans, Robots, and the Future

Isaac Asimov died in 1992, before ASIMO, the DARPA Grand Challenge, and the first nanobots had come into existence. But in 1979, in an essay titled "Intelligences Together," he foreshadowed the idea that humans and robots may never think alike but will still be able to cooperate. Asimov wrote:

> Each variety of intelligence has its advantages and, in combination, human intelligence and computer intelligence—each filling in the gaps and compensating for the weaknesses of the other—can advance far more rapidly than either one could alone. It will not be a case of completing and replacing at all, but of intelligences together, working more efficiently than either could alone within the laws of nature.

Asimov predicted a golden future of human-computer, or human-robot, partnership. Closer to the present, however, some people would simply be glad to have a robot that could walk the dog, guard the house, water the garden, remind grandmother to take her pills, and wash the dishes, the car, and the windows. Will a robot really be able to do all that? How soon?

In his 1998 book *Robot: Mere Machine to Transcendent Mind,* roboticist Hans Moravec of Carnegie Mellon University speculated about

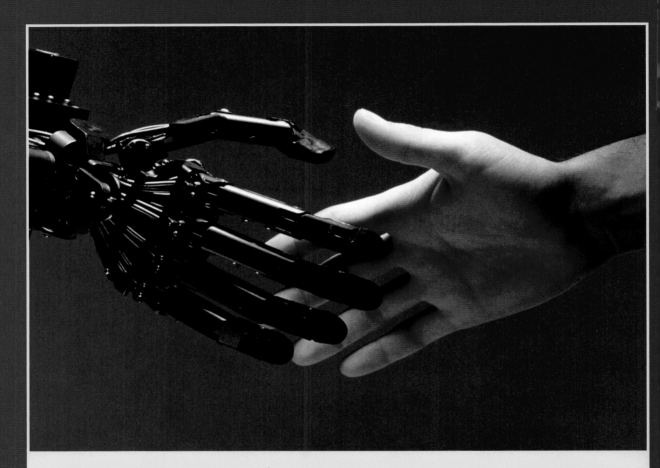

WILL HUMAN BEINGS AND ROBOTS COOPERATE IN THE FUTURE? THE GROWING FIELD OF ROBOETHICS IS CONCERNED WITH HOW WE WILL TREAT ROBOTS IN THE COMING YEARS. SOME ROBOTICS RESEARCHERS HAVE ALSO SPECULATED ABOUT HOW THEY WILL TREAT US.

possible trends in robotics, from the coming decades to the distant future. In Moravec's opinion, the science and art of robotics is now "like a baby poised for sudden change." He predicted that general-purpose household and utility robots will start to become available during the first quarter of the twenty-first century. Such robots will be mobile and able to perform a variety of chores in the home; they will be genuinely useful, not simply entertaining novelties.

The next step after robot domestic workers might be robots that could serve as office receptionists or clerks, or as service employees in such settings as restaurants, resorts, and hospitals and clinics. These jobs require a degree of interaction with humans that many roboticists think is decades away. Still, when the technology is available, employers might well decide that the virtues of such a worker—mistake-proof, always on duty, never surly—more than offset the initial cost of purchasing it. What effect will the advent of such machines have on our social, economic, and political systems? If a lot of people are displaced from their jobs in a short period of time, widespread unemployment could cause economic distress, and perhaps worse. Will robots widen the gap between society's haves and have-nots? Will people riot in the streets against the new robot cashiers and waiters, as silk workers in eighteenth-century Lyon rioted against Vaucanson's semiautomated looms?

Perhaps robots will be introduced into the workforce gradually enough for individuals and the national and world economy to adjust to them. That prospect, however, raises another question: If robots are going to do more and more jobs, including highly skilled ones like building robots and performing surgery, what are people going to do? The entire population cannot become research scientists, or ballet dancers, or poets. If robot workers give us more and more free time, how will we fill it? Based on current trends, some might suspect that the human race, once relieved of the need to work, might spend all of its time surfing the Internet and watching television.

"Barring cataclysm," Moravec says, "I consider the development of intelligent machines a near-term inevitability." The widespread use of workbots could raise pressing questions of employment and social policy even if those robots were not particularly intelligent. Machine intelligence, however, raises other questions—philosophical and ethical ones. If robots are as intelligent as we are, are they our equals? How should we treat them?

Such questions go beyond the realm of pure intelligence, of manipulating information and solving problems. They enter the largely unknown territory called consciousness, or self-awareness. Consciousness is the mental activity or phenomenon by which you exist as a continuum of unique memories and characteristics, and through which you experience yourself "from inside." When you see a bird, for example, your brain does not simply register that you are seeing a bird—you also remember other birds you've seen, or wonder what kind of bird it is, or hope that it doesn't relieve itself on your windshield. Those somewhat random, highly personal reactions are functions of your consciousness. Another function of consciousness is the sensation we all have from time to time of seeming to watch our own thoughts, or examine our feelings.

Consciousness is basic to our existence, yet philosophers and brain scientists are still struggling to define and explain it. Debates about the ethical treatment of animals often revolve around questions of whether animals possess consciousness, and how much of it they possess. What would it mean if robots became conscious? Can a machine even become self-aware? Some people think that consciousness can arise only in organic, or flesh-and-blood, beings. Others speculate that self-awareness might develop in any sufficiently complex network that is set up to operate like a brain. For some people, such questions have a religious dimension. Is there such a thing as a soul, an essence that can only exist in a human mind? Could a conscious robot—a being created by humans and not by God—ever be said to have a soul?

What would it take to prove that a machine has become conscious? Doug Lenat's Cyc computer program calls itself "I," but that does not mean that it is self-aware, only that it is grammatical. If a robot starts

doing things that it was not programmed to do, does that mean that it has developed an independent will or merely that it is malfunctioning? The case of Gaak, the runaway robot, shows that appearances can be deceiving.

In 2002, Gaak was part of an exhibit at the Magna Science Center in Rotherham, England. Invented by Noel Sharkey of Sheffield University, the 2-foot-long (0.6-meter-long) robot was one of several "predatory robots" designed to feed on smaller, more nimble robots by sinking a "fang" into them and drawing off their power. The most successful predators were "mated"—in other words, their microchips were combined in new robots. Gaak was a product of this phase of the program. One day when the exhibit was left unattended for about fifteen minutes, Gaak crept through a gap in a barrier and made its way outside and across a parking lot. Near the exit from the science center onto a highway, Gaak was tripped up by sunlight shining through the leaves of trees. The dappled pattern of light and shade confused the robot's light-seeking sensors, causing it to go around and around in circles. A visitor to the science center found Gaak there and returned it to the exhibit, saying, "I knew Magna's robots interacted with each other, but I didn't expect to be greeted by one."

Sharkey explained Gaak's behavior as the result of its light-seeking program. "The predators can hallucinate seeing prey if you shine a light at them," he said. "A lot of light streams into Magna, and Gaak may have been chasing sunbeams." A simple mechanical explanation, right? Yet the urge to interpret Gaak's behavior in human terms was irresistible. Headlines and news articles about the incident led off with phrases such as "a robot's dash for freedom." Some of them referred to Gaak as "him." Our tendency to see our characteristics mirrored in even non-humanoid robots, coupled with projects such as Kismet and Cog that are meant to make robots' actions more humanlike, may make it difficult for us to draw a sharp line between machine and mind. And that, in turn, may make us question whether robots are our servants or our slaves.

The ethical treatment of robots is not an issue for the far future. Around the world today, people are discussing roboethics, as the new field of robot ethics is called. In 2006, a British government study of robotics included the prediction that within fifty years, robots could demand the same rights as humans. Will robots someday want to vote, or to be paid for their labor (perhaps in electricity)? Will abolition movements form to free robots from what some might call slavery?

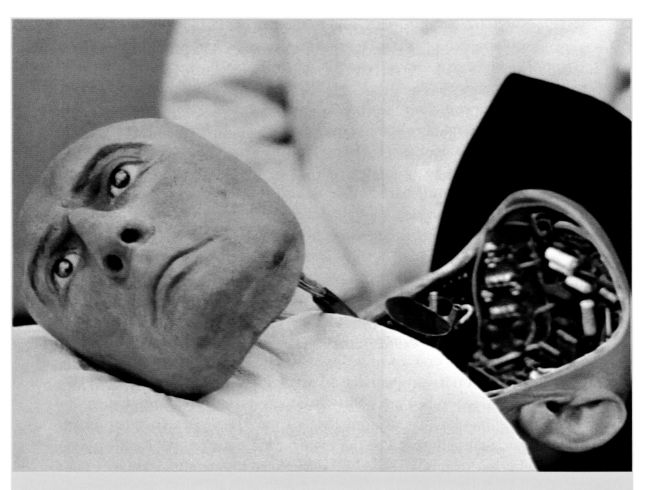

IN THE 1973 FILM *WESTWORLD*, A DEFECT IN AN ENTERTAINMENT ANDROID LEADS TO DISASTER.

The European Robotics Research Network is drawing up ethical guidelines for robotics research, similar to the guidelines that some nations have developed for other sciences with potential risks, such as nuclear engineering and genetic engineering. An early version of its report said, "In the 21st century humanity will coexist with the first alien intelligence we have ever come in contact with—robots. It will be an event rich in ethical, social, and economic problems."

WITH A BUILT-IN CAMERA AND MUSIC PLAYER, THE WOWWEE ROBOT IS A PRETTY ADVANCED TOY. OWNERS CAN PROGRAM IT TO MIMIC THEIR OWN VOICES AND EVEN THEIR PERSONALITIES—PERHAPS A SMALL FIRST STEP TOWARD A FUTURE IN WHICH HUMAN AND ROBOT QUALITIES MERGE?

system to process nerve signals, carry information, or stimulate muscles and other nerve endings. Steven Mann of the University of Toronto is moving in that direction. Mann has developed a pair of specially designed glasses that not only correct his vision but also allow him to surf the Internet, monitor his body's vital signs, and take video images of anything he sees. The glasses even let him create visual "nametags" for people he meets, so that the next time he sees them he can be sure of remembering their names. Mann hopes soon to develop an implantable version of his "visual memory prosthesis."

Supplementing our bodies with machinery could become easier and more common in the near future. The next step, say Kurzweil and some others, will be to leave our bodies entirely. If science can solve the riddles of consciousness, it may one day be possible to have our minds downloaded into information systems and transferred into durable, even immortal, machines. That prospect raises yet another question about humans and robots: If your thoughts, memories, and personality are placed in an artificial body, will that make you a robot? Or will it make the robot human?

**nanotechnology**—The science of designing and building extremely small technology, such as nanobots (tiny robots).

**patent**—A form of ownership that lets an inventor control, and profit from, the use of an invention for a set time in any country in which the patent is registered.

**proprioception**—Body awareness; an organism's ability to sense the position and orientation of its body.

**prototype**—The first model of something new.

**robot**—A reprogrammable, artificial, electronic-mechanical device that performs some human tasks; may or may not resemble a human being; usually has some ability to perceive and react to circumstances, move, manipulate objects, and act independently.

**robotics**—The study of robots; includes robotic engineering, the design and building of robots.

**sensors**—Instruments such as cameras, thermometers, microphones, and motion detectors that allow a robot to receive information about the world.

**teleoperation**—The act of controlling a telerobot or telerobotic arm or tool from a distance.

**telerobot**—A robot that is remotely controlled by a human operator through teleoperation.

# *Web Sites*

Some useful Web sites about robots are listed here. Since this book was written, some of these sites may have changed, moved to new addresses, or gone out of existence. New sites may now be available. In addition to these Web sites, many others also provide information about robots and robotics.

**ASIMO Home Page**
http://asimo.honda.com
Honda's humanoid robot, ASIMO, has its own Web page, with videos of the robot in action and a detailed but kid-friendly account of its design and construction.

**Building Your First Robot**
http://www.robotics.com/arobot/build.html
This site explains the basic steps in designing and building a simple robot and offers tips on material, problem-solving, and additional information resources.

**History of Robotics**
http://www.faculty.ucr.edu/~currie/roboadam.htm
A sixth-grader's prizewinning Web site about robotics presents an illustrated history, a section on robots in the news, and many links to outside resources.

### Robot Bomb Squad

http://www.pbs.org/wgbh/nova/robots/

This online supplement to a PBS *Nova* program about robots explores their use in hazardous jobs; also included are video clips and ideas about possible future robots.

### Robot Building Lessons

http://www.cs.cmu.edu/~chuck/infopg/roboinfo.html

Roboticist Chuck Rosenberg offers insight and advice on the challenges of building a robot.

### Robot Hall of Fame

http://www.robothalloffame.org/

Created in 2003 by Carnegie Mellon University, the Robot Hall of Fame honors both real and fictional robots that have made significant contributions to robotics and culture. Among the robots that have been inducted into the Hall of Fame are R2D2, Shakey, ASIMO, and Maria from *Metropolis*.

### Robot Information Central

http://www.robotics.com/robots.html

This Web page's table of contents has links to dozens of sites on topics such as robots in the movies and robots in space; it also contains sections on many robot games and contests.

### Robotics

http://www.robotics.utexas.edu/rrg/learn_more/history/

The Robotics Research Group at the University of Texas in Austin maintains this overview of robots and robotics.

### Robotics

http://www.thetech.org/robotics/universal/index.html

The Tech Museum of Innovation's online Robotics exhibit includes a video interview with robotics researcher Hans Moravec and useful summaries of more than a dozen topics, including how robots are made, what they do, and how they may be used in the future.

## Robotics Lab

http://robotics.megagiant.com/index.html

This kid-friendly site focuses on learning about and building simple robots; it has an extensive menu of links to informative sites and videos.

## Robots

http://www.livescience.com/robots/

This portal page is a useful, well-administered gateway to dozens of recent articles about robots in the news and advances in robotics.

## Rover Ranch

http://prime.jsc.nasa.gov/ROV/

NASA's Rover Ranch page is an introduction to robot engineering, with a Robots 101 course and online simulations that let users design and operate robots.

**FOR TEACHERS OR ADVANCED READERS**

Bekey, George A. *Autonomous Robots: From Biological Inspiration to Implementation and Control.* Cambridge, MA: MIT Press, 2005.

Bergren, Charles M. *Anatomy of a Robot.* New York: McGraw-Hill, 2003.

Cohen, John. *Human Robots in Myth and Science.* London: George Allen & Unwin, 1966.

Hornyak, Timothy N. *Loving the Machine: The Art and Science of Japanese Robots.* Tokyo, Japan: Kodansha, 2006.

Moravec, Hans. *Robot: Mere Machine to Transcendent Mind.* New York: Oxford University Press, 1998.

Roshein, Mark E. *Leonardo's Lost Robots.* New York: Springer, 2006.

Sandin, Paul. *Robot Mechanisms and Mechanical Devices Illustrated.* New York: McGraw-Hill, 2003.

Severin, E. Oliver. *Robot Companions.* New York: McGraw-Hill, 2004.

Stone, Brad. *Gear Heads: The Turbulent Rise of Robotic Sports.* New York: Simon & Schuster, 2003.

Williams, Karl. *Build Your Own Humanoid Robots.* New York: McGraw-Hill, 2004.

Wood, Gaby. *Edison's Eve: A Magical History of the Quest for Mechanical Life.* New York: Knopf, 2002.

# Index

Page numbers in **boldface** are illustrations, tables, and charts.

# About the Author

Rebecca Stefoff has written numerous nonfiction books for readers of all ages. Her works include biographies of historical and literary figures as well as books about science, nature, and exploration. Stefoff has written about inventions and their effects in other volumes of the Great Inventions series, including *The Telephone*, *Microscopes and Telescopes*, and *Submarines*. She is also the author of the ten-volume Benchmark Books series North American Historical Atlases, as well as the five-volume series World Historical Atlases. You can find more information about her books for young readers at http://www.rebeccastefoff.com.